The Financial Post

INVESTING IN

GOLD

HOW TO OWN IT, HOW TO PROFIT FROM IT

JONATHAN GOODMAN, NED GOODMAN AND STEVEN G. KELMAN

KEY PORTER BOOKS

Canadian Cataloguing in Publication Data
Goodman, Ned, date
   Investing in gold

ISBN 1-55013-301-2

1. Gold.   2. Metals as an investment.   I. Kelman,
Steven G. (Steven Gershon), 1945–   . II. Goodman,
Jonathan, date.   III. Title.

HG293.K45 1992   332.63   C90-095348-9

Key Porter Books Limited
70 The Esplanade
Toronto, Ontario
Canada   M5E 1R2

Typesetting: Computer Composition of Canada Inc.
Printed and bound in Canada

   93 94 95 96   6 5 4 3 2

Contents

Preface / vii
Acknowledgments / ix
Introduction / 1

I. Inflation and Gold / 7
    1. The Relationship Between Inflation
        and Gold / 13
    2. The Real Value of Gold / 34
    3. The Next 10 Years / 42
    4. Gold Will Almost Certainly Double in
        Price / 47

II. Supply and Demand / 53
    5. The Supply of Gold / 61
    6. The Demand for Gold / 90

III. How to Invest in Gold / 105
    7. Using Gold Effectively / 107
    8. Owning Bullion / 128
    9. Investing in Shares / 140
    10. How to Buy Gold Mutual Funds and
         Closed-end Gold Funds / 161
    11. Options and Futures / 184
    12. The Outlook for Gold / 203

Glossary / 211
Index / 227

Preface

A month ago an anonymous business writer noted the forthcoming publication of this book and bellowed that the authors, as investors in gold and as managers of gold funds, had a vested interest in making sure that gold prices moved higher. I have been a follower of gold markets during my entire business career, which spans 30 years. In that time, I am on record as having been a long-term bull, a roaring bull, a cautious bull, a significant seller of gold as it approached the lofty heights of $800 U.S. per ounce, and, in more recent years, a cautious and a long-term bull as we approach the end of a 12-year bear market in the price of gold bullion.

At this moment in time, when most economic pundits perceive world inflation rates to be generally under control, I can classify myself once again as a roaring bull on gold.

With that said, is it any wonder that my personal

portfolio is heavily weighted in gold stocks; or that, as investment counselors, we are recommending that our clients maintain a heavy precious metal and gold weighting? Is it any wonder that, as the marketer of a precious metals mutual fund, Dynamic Precious Metals Ltd., and as the manager of BGR Precious Metals Inc., we are telling our unit-holders and shareholders and anyone else that this is a good time to buy gold?

Our view is that the bear market for gold is just about spent. Probably before this book is even printed and distributed, a new bull market for gold will emerge. As we explain in later chapters of this book, the dramatic rise of the price of gold will be a direct reflection of the reflation that will have to occur in order to save the world from absolute deflation and depression.

An inflationary increase in world money supply will occur at exactly the time that the newly mined supply of gold will plateau and decline. This lack of new supply during an inflationary period, coupled with growing demand for gold in the form of gold jewelry, will create the disequilibrium necessary to achieve the forecast of a doubling in the price of gold.

With this in mind, we don't believe that we are in conflict when we put our money where our mouths are. This book will tell you why we have done so.

Ned Goodman

Acknowledgments

There are several individuals whose help was sought in the preparation of this book and we would like to thank them for their contributions: James R. Blakely; Christopher Brown, Bunting Warburg Inc.; our colleague John Budden; Frank Holmes, United Services Advisors Inc.; Seymour Friedland, York University; Mike Simms, Nesbitt Thomson Inc.; Tony Walsh, International Corona Corporation; the Geneva and New York offices of the World Gold Council; and the gold departments of the Bank of Nova Scotia, the Canadian Imperial Bank of Commerce, and the Toronto Dominion Bank. In addition, we would like to thank Gold Fields Mineral Services Ltd., publishers of the industry statistical bible *Gold 1992*, and its chief executive, Stewart Murray, for permission to use their copyright material in the preparation of several of our charts and tables. We would also like to thank our assistants,

Helene Edwards and Leslie Murray, for keeping track of our files and for their comments on early drafts of the book; our editor, Jennifer Glossop, for making the book more readable; and our families, for their patience.

Introduction

Little more than two decades ago, the price of gold was $35 (U.S.) an ounce. By January 1980 speculative buying had pushed it to a record $850 an ounce. Since then gold has been in a bear or falling market, and by mid-1992 was trading below $340 an ounce. What do the nineties hold for gold? We feel that the bear market is ending and that gold will be one of the better-performing assets of the 1990s.

Gold remains an essential part of every investment portfolio for a number of reasons. It does not devalue during periods of inflation as does paper currency. When included with other types of assets in a portfolio, it tends to stabilize rates of return. In periods of financial crisis and political turmoil it can be easily stored and transported. In periods of rising gold prices, gold and gold shares can be used by speculators seeking returns far above those available from other securities.

Gold is a mirror of the world's economic history. It has been a measure of national and personal wealth for thousands of years and has been a medium of exchange for more than 6,000 years.

It is an investment available to virtually everyone. Investors with only a few spare dollars can buy gold coins from banks or invest in a portfolio of gold and gold securities managed professionally through gold mutual funds. Wealthy investors can buy bullion or mutual funds or build a portfolio of gold shares. In addition there are gold futures contracts and gold options. Futures contracts are agreements to deliver or accept delivery of a specific amount of a commodity at a specified date at a firm price agreed upon at the time the contract was made. Options contracts are rights to buy or sell a commodity at a specific price up to a specified date, but unlike futures they are not obligations. Sophisticated investors can use futures and options to increase portfolio returns and protect themselves against wide price swings. Speculators can use futures and options, or purchase gold with borrowed funds, in the hope of making high returns.

Most gold producers use what are called "derivatives" to sell forward part or all of their production. By selling forward they sell gold that they will produce in subsequent years at a price moderately higher than today's, in effect locking in a premium price. Similarly, gold users such as jewelry manufacturers can use derivatives to lock in the price they will later pay for gold.

Nations can and do use gold as reserves to finance their international trade and to back a portion of their paper currencies or their debt.

Many analysts and economists have recently claimed that gold has lost its purpose. Certainly the performance of the gold market during the Persian Gulf war disillusioned many investors. The failure of gold prices to soar during the war left them wondering if gold does truly provide a hedge against inflation, deflation, and currency crises. These detractors, for the most part, were probably never real believers in gold. They probably never accepted gold as the only form of money that isn't an obligation or liability of a government, or as a precious commodity of which even small quantities have significant value and which has served for more than 6,000 years as the world's savings through political and economic turmoil. They point to how the currency crises in Eastern Europe and the former Soviet Union have not had the commonly expected result of raising the price of gold bullion and to how during the Gulf war the gold price in fact went down. They talk glibly and without knowledge about how the price of gold has not kept pace with world-wide inflation. Further, they argue, inflation is no longer a problem and, consequently, the price of gold should not be expected to do anything other than remain stagnant or decline further. They are wrong. Gold, in fact, has done all that it traditionally has

been expected to. Followers of the stock market can
easily see that bullion was the stellar performer
during 1990 when its price was relatively steady
while virtually all the world's stock markets declined — some dramatically (see figure 1). Certainly,
anyone who held currencies of Eastern European
countries, the Soviet ruble, the Brazilian cruzeiro,
or the Iraqi dinar would rather have held gold bullion.

In fact, most wealthy people in Eastern Europe,
the Soviet Union, Brazil, and Iraq probably held at
least part of their savings in gold bullion, and some
of them certainly liquidated their savings in order
to leave and live. Those without gold savings were

**Figure 1: Relative Returns of Bullion and Major World
Stock Markets in 1990**

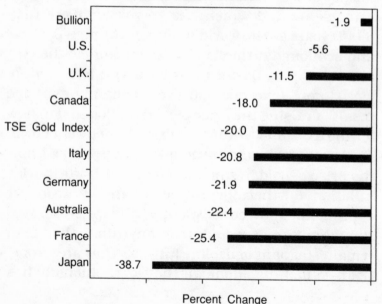

	Percent Change
Bullion	-1.9
U.S.	-5.6
U.K.	-11.5
Canada	-18.0
TSE Gold Index	-20.0
Italy	-20.8
Germany	-21.9
Australia	-22.4
France	-25.4
Japan	-38.7

left penniless and stranded. It is a better-than-even-money bet that Saddam Hussein has a significant gold hoard in a safe haven.

Figure 2, which compares the value of the Brazilian cruzeiro with the price of gold during the past decade, shows clearly why gold is hoarded in Brazil and why the Brazilian government pays a premium price to purchase it from its citizens. Undoubtedly Brazilians who held gold did better than those holding their own currency.

Gold still has a purpose. This book is about that purpose — its history and its future. We believe that the price of gold should double to around $700 an ounce in U.S. funds by the year 2000 because of completely normal supply and demand market forces (all gold prices are quoted in U.S. funds unless specified otherwise). We further believe that a confluence of isolated events some time in the next three to five years may cause the price of gold to achieve that target even earlier. Moreover, there is a reasonable chance that our target price of $700 an ounce will be exceeded during the forecasted period.

Our conclusions are based not on an emotional attachment to gold but on an analysis of its long-term investment advantages. We do not foresee Armageddon. Indeed, we expect that events in the world will unfold as they have in the past. If, however, the expected happens, we expect gold to provide a hedge against the unknown.

Investing in Gold will help you understand why gold should be a cornerstone of your investment

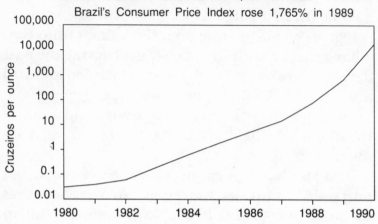

Figure 2: Gold's Price in Brazilian Cruzeiros
Brazil's Consumer Price Index rose 1,765% in 1989

portfolio and will show you how to invest in gold. The book is divided into three parts. The first explains the relationship between inflation and gold and looks at the outlook for gold for the next 10 years. The second covers supply and demand of gold bullion and shows how changes in the relationship point to higher gold prices. The third part is about investing in gold and explains choices investors have when investing in gold — bullion, certificates, coins, futures and options, gold stocks, and investment funds — and how each can be used to meet specific investment objectives. This section also explains the methods by which mining companies and industrial users can sell or buy gold.

I. Inflation and Gold

FROM AN INVESTMENT POINT OF VIEW, THE MAJOR reason to hold gold is to preserve wealth as real value over a very long time. Gold can, of course, be held as a speculative investment based on anticipated price increases, and many people have purchased gold and gold shares expecting to make huge profits over the short term. Even so, gold is the only long-term investment that has proved to be a protection against inflation and, at the same time, to be portable, tradable virtually every place on the globe, and recognized universally as a store of value — as money that cannot be created or destroyed by government. No other commodity can substitute for gold. It is highly liquid, hard to find, impossible to create, and its beauty has been cherished for centuries.

"You have a choice between trusting the natural stability of gold and the honesty and intelligence of the members of the government. And with all due respect to these gentlemen, I advise you, as long as the capitalist system lasts, vote for gold." Although these comments by George Bernard Shaw were directed at capitalism, they are just as applicable to communism, to monarchies, and to virtually every other political-economic system that has ever existed. Indeed, throughout economic history, government after government has attempted to create wealth out of air by cutting the gold content of its coins, or in recent times by printing more money, devaluing or reducing the purchasing power of the currency.

The story is as old as history. It starts when gov-

ernment needs more money to finance its operations than it can raise through taxes and through
borrowing. To stretch its wealth farther, the government creates money. It can do this in two ways.
It can make coins with a lower precious-metal content, or it can crank up the press and print more
paper money. Both these methods are attempts to
create wealth out of nothing, and both simply lead
to an adjustment of prices to reflect the reduced
value of the currency. This situation leads to inflation.

Because of the coins' reduced gold content, more
are needed to purchase the same amount of goods
or services than before the devaluation. Inflation,
taken to its extreme, can lead to the collapse of a
currency, as it did in Germany in 1923, or to a
major depression, as it did in the 1930s.

As long as there has been money, governments
have been debasing it. As recently as the mid-
1960s, the United States and Canada stopped using
silver in their coins. But the rulers of the Greek city
states were perhaps the first to try to increase their
wealth by cutting the gold and silver content of
coins. The city states of ancient Greece debased
their coinage to finance wars. And although the
economic ''law'' that bad money drives out good is
commonly attributed to Sir Thomas Gresham, who
lived during the reign of Elizabeth I, Aristophanes,
the ancient Greek playwright and satirist, said es-
sentially the same thing during the Peloponnesian
Wars.

In 216 B.C. Rome cut the copper content of its

coins in half in an attempt to stretch its military spending in its war against Carthage, and several Roman emperors debased their gold coins, in effect devaluing their currencies or revaluing precious metals. When Julius Caesar reigned, 40 gold aurei were coined from a pound of gold. Augustus increased it to 45. Nero continued the trend. By the time of Constantine, three centuries later, the aureus was being coined at the rate of 72 to the pound of gold, and the debasement of the Roman currency contributed to the fall of the empire.

After the collapse of the Roman Empire, Europe fell into disarray, with no central authority. Merchants no longer had faith in coins, and transactions were based on weight, just as they had been in Egypt and Sumer more than 2,000 years earlier. Trade declined and generally languished for hundreds of years.

The Crusades, however, brought about a major change. The Crusaders brought back huge amounts of gold and silver captured from the Byzantines and others. This new wealth encouraged the development of trade, and Britain, France, and other European countries introduced bimetal currency systems, which used silver as well as gold, and in fixed proportions. While commerce grew, its growth was restricted by the amount of gold available. The supply of gold had not changed much since Roman times, and trade, other than through barter, was largely tied to the supply of gold and silver. Columbus's discovery of America in 1492 changed the picture. Within a generation, Spain had conquered

Mexico and Peru. The pillage of the Americas resulted in massive flows of gold to Spain and then
through Europe as trade increased and debts were
paid. The sudden inflow of huge amounts of gold
into the European economy caused massive inflation as the new wealth pushed up prices of goods.

Within countries where the monarch had the
power to mint the coin of the realm, kings, like governments everywhere, never seemed to have enough
gold. They tried to increase their wealth by cutting
the gold and silver content of their coins. The trend
continued through the early 1700s, when Britain
pegged its currency to gold, establishing a stability
that, except during the Napoleonic Wars, lasted almost two centuries, until the First World War, when
nations abandoned the discipline of gold and instead printed money to finance their war efforts.

Figure 3: The Trend of Gold is Upward

**Since 1200 A.D. gold has advanced from $4.45 to $35
an ounce in New York funds.**

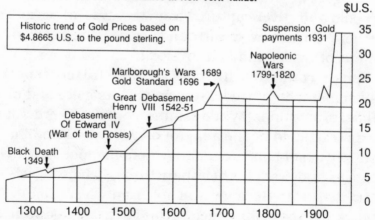

Source: The Financial Post, July 27, 1946

1. The Relationship Between Inflation and Gold

There are numerous ways to define inflation, but basically it means that money has lost its power. Inflation occurs when the money supply grows faster than the supply of goods and services, or as one popular definition puts it, when there is too much money chasing too few goods. The consequences of inflation are that the value of money declines and more units than previously are needed to purchase goods and services.

In North America today, money supply is the actual currency issued by governments and deposits, which are the supply of money created by the banking system. North American commercial banking institutions have the ability to create demand deposits by making loans and investments. These deposits, along with government-issued currency, act as the money supply of the economy. The financial system of a country tries to increase the money supply enough to allow for economic expansion without encouraging inflation. In reality, however, economies move in cycles that include periods of rising prices and periods of declining prices — inflation and deflation.

The problem is that what determines the total supply of money that people have to spend depends on two government policies that are often at odds with each other — price stability and full employment. The main goal of the central banks in our system (the Federal Reserve in the United States and the Bank of Canada in Canada) is to maintain a monetary policy that provides a currency that can be trusted. In other words, the objective is to provide a currency that investors can count on to be a stable store of value, or at least to not lose its value over time. Any market economy requires, above all else, price stability. Without price stability people will put their money into other assets that retain value. Thus, during the past two decades, concerns about inflation in North America led to flights of capital into the stock market, commodities, precious metals, and real estate.

As the citizens of the countries that make up the former Soviet Union and Eastern Europe have recently discovered, a free-market economy requires confidence in a country's money. For a capitalistic market economy and democratic system to work at their best, sound money or at least the perception of sound money is absolutely essential.

Unfortunately, our political system works against the concept of sound money. Politicians, hoping to be elected to office, make promises to the electorate which they cannot afford to keep. Then, in office, they spend money the government doesn't have in order to get re-elected. When we look at world history and the cycles of inflation and deflation, it is clear that for a variety of reasons our leaders have consistently done a very poor job of regulating the supply of money. At times of recession or depression people have had so little money available, or they think they do, that they don't buy all the economy can produce. In the extreme, prices, profits, and employment decline, and production shrinks. The contraction of the economy halts only when prices are so low, or the supply of money so high, that there is, or is perceived to be, enough money available for the purchase of all the excess goods. Only at that point does the system once again operate efficiently.

Politicians or central bankers are often so worried about the possibility of recession, or about their own future if there is a recession, that they increase money supply in the hope of avoiding recession. The result is that inflation becomes a permanent fixture of the economy. Moreover, while governments occasionally make attempts to wring inflation out of the economy — generally after elections — such attempts are usually feeble because of the disruptions that would result from business failures, unemployment, and the sharp reduction of interest income should interest rates decline.

Given this centuries-old tendency toward inflation, and our fear of future inflation, it is not surprising that we turn to gold as an investment. As inflation rises, so does the price of gold.

The Gold Standard

As Europe and North America developed econom-ically in the nineteenth century, trade among coun-tries grew, and by the late 1800s most countries had adopted a gold standard. Britain had intro-duced its gold standard in the mid-1800s, when it made the pound fully convertible, or exchangeable, into gold for both domestic and international trade. The system encouraged commerce, and other coun-tries adopted similar systems.

Simply put, with a gold standard, money and gold are the same. The government's liabilities (paper money) are backed by gold on a one-for-one basis. Banks can issue currency only against their gold holdings or against holdings of government bonds, which in turn are backed by gold. In effect, the growth of the economy and the growth of credit are tied to the availability of gold. In actual fact, though, paper money was not backed on a one-for-one basis. Rather, each unit of currency was only par-tially backed by gold. However, changes in the total amount of money — defined as currency plus de-posits — increased or decreased roughly in propor-tion to changes in the amount of gold held by that country.

All international transactions were settled in gold. Therefore, countries that were most efficient and were able to provide the lowest-cost goods were net exporters and built their gold reserves. Less-efficient countries became net importers and had their gold reserves reduced.

Since gold was money, a reduction in gold holdings was a reduction in money supply — in effect a squeeze on credit. Such a reduction could cause loans to be called, and lead to unemployment and lower prices. The resulting recession would cut demand for imports as well as for domestic goods, and industry, now likely becoming more cost competitive, would be able to produce goods for export, correcting the deficit.

The gold standard was far from perfect. Because money supply was based on gold, economic cycles were tied to the flow of gold in and out of a nation. As a result, economic cycles could be severe. Nevertheless, the system worked fairly well from the 1880s to the First World War for several reasons. World trade was relatively small by today's standards. Governments had yet to establish large-scale systems of tariff barriers. Governments were not in the business of controlling or managing their economies. Peacetime budgets were balanced. Some countries did, in fact, build foreign-exchange reserves as well as gold reserves in order to manage their economies. However, the effect on the international system was only minor.

The gold standard broke down during the First World War, when gold flowed out of Europe to pay for war materials and paper money was printed to fuel the domestic economy. In the years after the war, most European currencies fell dramatically against gold and were exchangeable for a fraction of the gold they had been worth before the war. Germany's currency lost all its value in 1923 in a bout of hyperinflation as money was printed without any backing.

The Gold Exchange Standard

Immediately after the First World War the world's ability to reestablish international trade was stifled by the poor state of the foreign-exchange markets. Recognizing that stable exchange markets were necessary for the expansion of trade and Europe's economic recovery, world monetary authorities decided to develop a new system of converting currencies and restoring stability to the world monetary system.

It was not an easy task. To return currencies to their prewar parities against gold would have caused massive credit deflation. Governments would have had to reduce the money supply dramatically to raise the purchasing power of currencies to prewar values, a solution that was totally unacceptable to the authorities. Consequently, they decided to permit central banks to use foreign-exchange reserves as well as gold and government bonds as the basis on which nations could create money. The idea was that currencies that were convertible into gold, such as the pound sterling, were as good as gold, even though the currencies were only partially backed by gold. This decision brought about the "gold exchange standard" in 1922. Under it, central banks held paper gold — reserve currencies — in addition to gold holdings. These secondary reserves were left on deposit in British and U.S. banks or invested in British and U.S. government bonds earning interest. Under the gold exchange standard it was no longer necessary to ship gold to settle international trade liabilities. Rather, currencies were transferred. Countries could increase their money supply by adding to the reserve currencies in their central banks.

In 1922 the major reserve currency was the pound sterling. But the United States with its buoyant economy was the banker to the world. In theory the gold exchange standard should have worked. But it was not self-correcting, as was the gold standard. A country adding, say, dollars as a reserve currency would increase its money supply just as if it had gold. But there was no corresponding decrease in the money supply in the reserve currency country. The country using, say, dollars as a reserve currency would keep those dollars on deposit in New York, where they would become part of the U.S. money supply as well. Some countries, in fact, expanded their domestic money supplies, paying no heed to the level of reserves, and ended up with double- and even triple-digit inflation rates. To preserve foreign-exchange reserves, these countries restricted the convertibility of their currencies by placing limits on the number of dollars individuals or companies could exchange each year for travel or by making it illegal to hold hard currencies. To make it difficult for citizens of such countries to preserve the value of their money by purchasing consumer goods, high import duties were put in place. Black markets to convert currencies usually developed, and the true value of the currency was often reflected in the black market exchange rate. Countries that place restrictions on the convertibility of their currencies are called "soft currency countries" as opposed to hard currency countries, such as the United States and Canada, which place no restrictions on currency convertibility.

The success of the gold exchange standard depended on the willingness of a reserve currency nation — such as the United Kingdom — to preserve the value of its currency against gold. To do this the country whose currency was used as a reserve had to maintain a stable currency, even if it meant sacrificing its domestic economic policies. If, instead, it opted for economic growth, inflation would be the result. As the value of its currency would be reduced, holders of that currency would become concerned about its continued convertibility and would convert it to gold, reducing the gold reserves of the reserve currency country.

The gold exchange standard tended to encourage inflation for another reason as well. The country supplying the reserve currency would not necessarily reduce the amount of capital available for domestic use by the amount provided for foreign use. In effect, therefore, the gold was used as currency backing more than once, and the amount of money created by this gold exceeded the gold's value.

European currencies stabilized in the 1920s, helped by heavy holdings of foreign-exchange in central banks. At the same time the use of credit was expanding and inflationary pressures were building. As the German and French economies recovered, they attracted significant foreign investment, which in turn caused inflationary pressures in those countries. Because inflation threatened the value of their currencies, Germany and France started converting their foreign-exchange reserves into gold in the hope that this would stabilize the value of the mark and franc. However, their sales of sterling for gold pushed the value of the pound down. To strengthen the pound, the Bank of England tightened credit, cooling the already depressed British economy.

The United States had been the major supplier of capital to an expanding European economy. But with its own economy expanding and needing capital, the flows reversed and the United States became an importer, rather than an exporter, of capital. With capital flowing out of Europe, central banks tightened their monetary policies, to raise interest rates, in an attempt to support the values of their currencies. But pressure on the pound continued, and concerns about its future resulted in central banks converting their pounds and other foreign-exchange reserves into gold reserves. Foreign-exchange reserves had been growing between 1924 and 1928 at a much greater pace than gold reserves. So, when the credit crunch began, paper gold rather than bullion represented the bulk of reserves.

Liquidity, or the ease with which money could be

borrowed, declined and short-term interest rates rose. In 1929, the U.S. stock market, which had soared because of easy credit and speculation, collapsed. In an attempt to protect domestic economies, many countries threw up tariff walls and introduced import quotas.

The liquidity crisis, or credit squeeze, continued for several years. In 1931 Austria's largest commercial bank, the Credit Anstalt, failed. The Austrian schilling plunged in value against gold despite attempts to support it. The German mark fell next. The selling spread to the pound. In September 1931 the Bank of England suspended the pound's convertibility into gold. It did not have enough gold to meet even a fraction of its liabilities to foreign creditors.

The U.S. dollar was under pressure as well. In April 1933 the American government stopped all gold exports, and by executive order, nationalized gold, requiring its citizens to turn in their gold for currency and prohibiting its ownership in the United States. While banks turned in their gold coins, many coins were hoarded by individuals who were not deterred by the penalties. Eventually the rules were changed to allow possession of U.S. gold coins by collectors.

On January 31, 1934, the United States devalued its currency against gold by 71 percent, setting a price of $35 an ounce (gold had traded at $20.67 since 1834) and allowing convertibility once again (but not for its own citizens). While $35 an ounce fairly valued gold relative to the dollar, the world's perception was that because the Depression had brought down prices in the United States, gold was overvalued. As a result, gold flowed into the United States from foreign sources, swelling U.S. reserves, which peaked at some 654 million ounces in 1950. This massive gold hoard allowed the United States to dominate world economic events through the 1950s and 1960s.

Bretton Woods and the Postwar Years

In 1944, when victory over the Axis powers was in sight, it was apparent that the international monetary system had to be reconstructed after the excessive inflation of the war years, and that the new system had to avoid the mistakes that helped bring about the Great Depression.

The Bretton Woods Conference established the financial system the West would use in the postwar period. It reestablished the gold exchange standard and the use of reserve currencies, in particular the U.S. dollar because of its gold reserves and economic strength. As well, it led to the formation of the International Monetary Fund to provide a mechanism for stabilizing major currencies in times of crisis and to act as a watchdog over the regulators — a toothless watchdog, as history has shown.

The experience of the depression was still very fresh in the minds of governments in the early postwar period, and economic policy was designed to provide full employment, keep prices and currencies relatively stable, avoid another depression, and smooth out or even eliminate business cycles. These objectives were to be accomplished by adjusting government spending. If the economy looked as if it was slowing, government spending was to be increased to stimulate demand, even if it meant the government ran a deficit. And if the economy was expanding too quickly, the government was to cut its spending to cool demand and build a budget surplus.

However, in reality, government spending policies, at least in Canada and the United States, seem to be tied more to the election cycle than to the business cycle, with spending increasing before an election, and cutbacks, if any, following elections. Moreover, since the 1950s, governments have increasingly introduced social benefit programs at a cost beyond what can be supported by taxes. The result is that governments have continuous deficits rather than surpluses and the objectives of a balanced budget or a surplus have been replaced by a new objective — reducing the deficit. Governments obtain the additional funds they need by borrowing. And because there generally isn't enough money in the economy to meet the borrowing needs of government, corporations, and individuals, government deficits have largely been financed by expanding the money supply at a pace in excess of economic growth or productivity. As money supply has expanded, the portion of it that is backed by gold has obviously contracted.

At the same time as government debt has risen, personal and corporate debt has soared as a result of easy credit and continuing deregulation of the banking industry. Moreover, the increasing globalization of the banking system has limited the ability of individual countries to cool inflation by curbing credit through higher interest rates or slower money supply growth. These measures do nothing to stop corporations from borrowing internationally in other currencies, whether U.S. dollars, Swiss francs, yen, or marks.

The 1970s and 1980s

In the late 1970s, inflation seemed out of control. Interest rates barely kept pace with inflation. On an after-tax basis, real rates of return from treasury bills were negative. The price of gold soared, reaching a peak in January 1980 at $850 an ounce. In 1980 the U.S. inflation rate rose to 13 percent. The U.S. inflation bout of the late 1970s was eliminated in the early 1980s by the unprecedented rise in interest rates implemented by Paul Volcker, then head of the U.S. Federal Reserve. This surge in rates brought about the very significant recession of 1980–82.

By the mid-1980s, after soaring interest rates cooled the economy into recession, inflation fell to the 4–6 percent range, levels that continue today. In fact, these rates of inflation are now considered reasonable. Consumers, investors, and bankers have learned to live and work with them. Most people, however, have forgotten that in 1973, when President Richard Nixon invoked wage and price controls, inflation was deemed to be "out of control," and yet it was running at what was then con-

Figure 4: U.S. Treasury Bill Rates 1970–1991

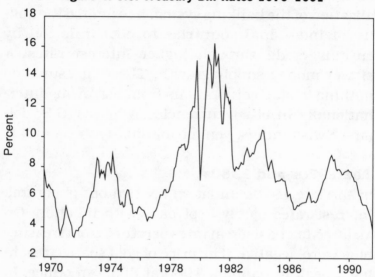

sidered a lofty and frightening 4 percent annual rate.

During the 1980s, an inflation rate below 10 percent was thought acceptable as long as the negative effect of inflation was offset through indexing, and many labor contracts did include clauses that provided a cost-of-living increase indexed to the consumer price index. Similarly, some loan agreements called for payment of a rate of interest that was in effect a combination of two rates: the inflation rate plus a real rate, which was the cost of the loan before inflation. Currency exchange rates can also be fine-tuned to reflect the effects of inflation and can be adjusted against the currencies of other trading nations with similar inflation. In fact, the weighted average inflation rate for the 24 nations that are members of the Organization for Economic Cooperation and Development (the OECD) is slightly higher than but surprisingly similar to the U.S. consumer price index (see figure 5).

The Cost of Inflation

Most people would agree that inflation becomes a major concern only when it rises to double-digit levels and begins to create fears about the future acceptability of paper money. A point to consider, however, is that both gold and paper money actually have no value in themselves. Their value derives only from the purposes for which they can be used. The key difference between paper and gold is

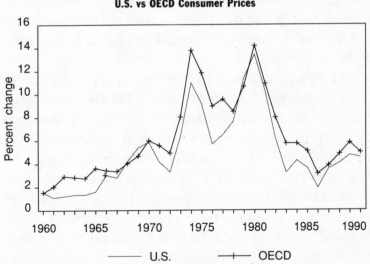

Figure 5: Annual Inflation
U.S. vs OECD Consumer Prices

that in times of double-digit inflation, money becomes highly suspect and gold is gold.

Constant inflation is harmful to the investment process in many ways. It pushes up the prices of assets, producing windfall gains. And while these gains are not real, they are taxed as real gains. Moreover, inflation makes for difficulties in accounting for corporate performance. As well, it distorts business decisions and limits corporate efficiency.

Most voters in North America were not hurt by the mild inflation of the 1980s. Some own assets, such as real estate, equities, and mutual funds, whose values have risen faster than the inflation rate. Others have benefited from interest rates that have exceeded the inflation rate. Government pensions have also risen with inflation. All in all, there was a perception of increasing wealth and well-being. Our politicians recognize that single-digit inflation with some consistency and stability will create an environment that will allow them to continue to be re-elected.

Yet many noted economists have repeatedly pointed out that, since the early 1960s, the United States has been on a path of economic self-destruction littered with credit crunches. The reliance on free markets leads to conflict between economic and political necessities. The requirement to get re-elected every four or five years has led to the repeated use of longer-term classical economic tools to solve short-term, large-size financial distortions. Inflation — the printing of money, or the increase of money supply in excess of productivity increases — is politically the most appealing method of solving the problem.

Most people will not accept short-term cuts in their standard of living to solve long-term problems. They will change their elected representatives and opt for the easier path of accepting a modicum of continuing inflation. Moreover, the American dream, with its democratic and social capitalism with free markets and free elections, has spread to Eastern Europe and the former Soviet Union. As we move into the twenty-first century, politicians all over the world want full employment for their electorate, along with the social welfare amenities that we all have learned to enjoy and now demand as mandatory.

Since 1982 we have been living with relatively low unemployment and "reasonable" inflation rates of 4 to 6 percent. Elected officials and central bankers believe that some inflation in the basic costs of living is not out of line, and that the costs of bringing down inflation to zero would be totally unacceptable. (Canada, in fact, did eliminate inflation — excluding inflation-reflecting items such as tobacco and alcohol tax increases — during 1991 at a cost that included permanent loss of jobs.)

It would therefore appear that a doubling of prices every 12 years (which is the result of 6 percent annual inflation) is politically acceptable to the electorate. The alternative, as some economists point out, is that to reduce the rate of inflation by one percentage point, the economy must run at four

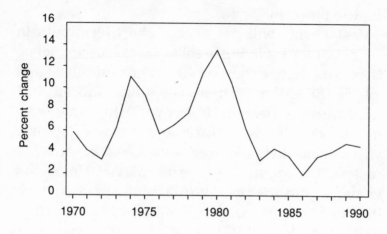

Figure 6: Annual Inflation
U.S. Consumer Price Index (1970–1990)

percentage points below its absolute capacity. From 1979 to 1982, the U.S. economy probably sacrificed close to 10 percent of its annual GNP in order to allow Mr. Volcker and the Federal Reserve to achieve some semblance of control over inflation. This decline in output was the result of a deliberate policy of tight money brought on by the Federal Reserve to control inflation. Except for a slight panic during 1981, when the Federal Reserve thought that it had lost control, it achieved its goal. The result, however, was that Jimmy Carter and the Democrats lost control of the White House in the next election. The electorate voted against unemployment and high interest rates and went with Ronald Reagan and George Bush for perceived short-term prosperity fueled by "supply side economics," but with only "mild" inflation of 4 to 6 percent.

Future politicians will not forget that lesson. Even though the official goal of the Federal Reserve and the Bush Administration is to achieve price stability by 1995, the experience of the 1980s quite clearly shows that reducing the rate of inflation even a little bit causes severe unemployment. (Indeed, the dangers of reducing inflation rates are clearly illustrated by the government of Canadian prime minister Brian Mulroney, which in 1991 had the lowest popularity of any government despite achieving the lowest inflation and interest rate levels in a generation.) In fact the cost of moving from current levels to zero inflation over the next five years would likely be an average annual U.S. unemployment rate of 8 percent. And governments facing reelection have historically been unwilling to make those economic decisions that would cut inflation at the cost of increasing unemployment.

The 1990s

There are some differences between the 1990s and the 1970s. Key is the change in demographics. Since the mid-1960s families have been having fewer children. As a result, fewer people will enter the workforce in the 1990s than did so in the 1970s and 1980s. No longer is there the pressure to create jobs as there was when the baby boomers entered the workforce. Similarly, no longer is there the pressure to build housing, a fact reflected in the end of the real estate boom, or beginning of the real

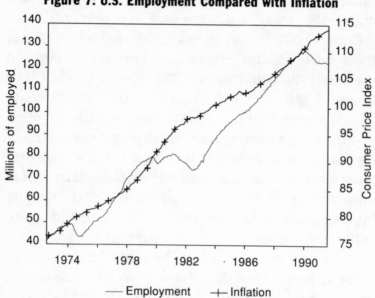

Figure 7: U.S. Employment Compared with Inflation

estate bust. Consequently, inflation rates should average lower in the 1990s than in the 1970s. Nevertheless, they are likely to be slightly higher than in the 1980s. The cost of debt servicing continues to grow, reflecting the increasing debt burden at all levels of government. Moreover, as the baby boomers age and approach retirement age there will be some pressures to maintain what has been perceived as high interest rates on deposits, and to provide or maintain expected income levels.

A major uncertainty, however, is the influence of the Federal Reserve's actions to end the recession or to prevent a depression. In mid-1992 it was apparent that the U.S. authorities had increased the

Figure 8: U.S. Money Supply (M1) Growth

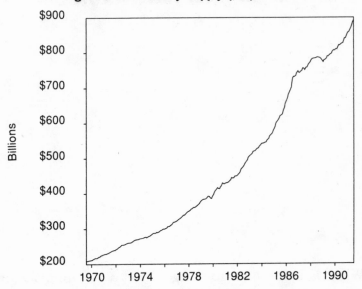

money supply rapidly since the beginning of the year. A continuation of this trend could send the inflation rate for the remainder of the decade significantly higher than it was in the 1980s. Similar situations have developed overseas. Germany, which for years served as the example of how inflation could be controlled, found its inflation rate heating up as unforeseen costs of unification led to higher money supply growth and, in turn, demand for higher wages from its powerful unions. Japan, too, has been having its economic problems, which might force its central bank to increase money supply in order to prop up the Japanese economy.

2. The Real Value of Gold

What is the real value of gold today — the price at which it should be trading? In figure 9, we have used the official gold price of 1879 (the beginning of the modern-day gold standards) and inflated it over the years by the most easily available inflation measurement statistics, the U.S. Wholesale Price Index from 1879 to 1919 and the U.S. Consumer Price Index from 1920 to 1990. As can be seen, the line representing the official price of gold and the line representing an inflation-adjusted gold value or real value meet only infrequently during a span of more than a century. From 1879 to 1933, the gold price was fixed at $20.67 an ounce. The real value of gold decreased during the deflationary years 1880–95, then increased dramatically as a result of inflation from 1895 to 1920. It plateaued during the stock market boom of 1920 to 1929, then fell during the deflationary period 1929–33. At that time

Figure 9: Price of Gold 1879–1991

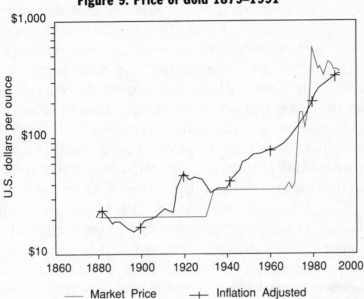

Market Price   Inflation Adjusted

the gold price was refixed at $35 an ounce as part of Franklin Delano Roosevelt's New Deal. (It is probably not coincidental that our calculations place the real value of gold at that time at $35.90 an ounce. We must assume that Roosevelt's officials used a process similar to ours in determining the $35 New Deal pegging.) The perception at that time was that by fixing gold at $35, the United States was intentionally valuing gold at too high a price. This premium price prompted global selling, allowing the United States to gather most of the world's gold from other countries at what history has proved to be a very attractive price.

The price remained fixed at $35 until 1967, when it was allowed to float in the open market. This occurred when our "real value" of gold was close to $100 an ounce. From 1967 to 1971, gold traded in a narrow range. Few investors were willing to go into the gold market because they were concerned that central banks intended to keep a ceiling on the price. But when President Nixon opened the gold window, and allowed U.S. citizens to once again own gold, the market price of gold began to rise substantially. Indeed, from 1974 to 1978, the actual price and "gold value" lines were in tandem.

The picture changed in the late 1970s and early 1980s, when the perception of continuing high inflation rates similar to those faced in the 1920s combined with free trading of gold caused gold to become excessively overvalued relative to our real-value benchmark.

The price of gold finally returned to its real-value benchmark only in 1990, where it rests today. Gold adjusted for U.S. inflation rates since 1879 had a real value in mid-1992 of about $370 an ounce.

It is interesting to note that the United States regularly buys and sells gold, albeit in small amounts. These purchases and sales are disclosed and often reported in such publications as the *Wall Street Journal*. In recent years reports indicate that the Federal Reserve has been a seller at prices above $400 an ounce and a buyer at around the $360 level. Similarly, the Bank of Canada acting as agent for the Government of Canada was a major seller of gold in 1991 and early 1992. These generally overlooked facts accompanied by recent bear raid muggings — selling of substantial amounts, driving the gold price lower — supposedly by Middle East speculators, leaves very suspicious fingerprints of central bank intervention in the free-market gold price. Rumors are easy to spread within the globally and broadly traded gold market, and central bankers are adept at using whatever means are necessary to maintain currency stability during times of severe political and financial crises.

It is important to remember that when the gold price was fixed at $35, the U.S. administration restricted private ownership of gold and, in fact, purchased gold only at that price. While gold was pegged at $35 an ounce, its real value rose through the second half of the 1930s and war years and reached $47 in 1944, when the Bretton Woods Agreement was installed. And in the mid-1970s, when the market price of gold soared in an unprecedented bull (rising) market, it did so in the face of continuous propaganda from central banks who actually sold gold at prices lower than market in an attempt to stem the speculative demand and to change the attendant perception that a rising gold price leaves in the minds of the electorate.

In 1983, President Reagan, himself a closet gold bug, successfully attacked the gold price because his administration was concerned that a rising gold price gave the wrong message about currency stability. A speculative burst in the gold price is a warning signal to the world that something serious is troubling the nation and its currency. The price of gold in a specific currency can be considered an index of that nation's currency stability. Alan

Greenspan, chairman of the U.S. Federal Reserve Board is well aware of this phenomenon. In 1966, he wrote an article entitled "Gold and Economic Freedom," stating:

The law of supply and demand is not to be conned. As the supply of money [of claims] increases relative to the supply of tangible assets in the economy, prices must eventually rise. Thus the earnings saved by the productive members of the society lose value in terms of goods. When the economy's books are finally balanced, one finds that this loss in value represents the goods purchased by the government for welfare or other purposes with the money proceeds of the government bonds financed by bank credit expansion.

In the absence of the gold standard, there is no way to protect savings from confiscation through inflation. There is no safe store of value. If there were, the government would have to make its holding illegal, as was done in the case of gold. If everyone decided, for example, to convert all his bank deposits to silver or copper or any other good, and thereafter declined to accept checks as payment for goods, bank deposits would lose their purchasing power and government-created bank credit would be worthless as a claim on goods. The financial policy of the welfare state requires that there be no way for the owners of wealth to protect themselves.

This is the shabby secret of the welfare statists' tirades against gold. Deficit spending is simply a scheme for the "hidden" confiscation of wealth. Gold stands in the way of this insidious process. It stands as a protector of property rights. If one grasps this, one has no difficulty in understanding the statists' antagonism toward the gold standard.

This article appeared in the *Objectivist* in July 1966 and was subsequently reprinted in Ayn Rand's 1967 book, *Capitalism: The Unknown Ideal*.

To derive our "real value" of gold, we used U.S. inflation statistics. Figure 10 shows the "real value" of gold based on the inflation statistics of the 24 members of the OECD. The United States accounts for almost half of the index. Nonetheless, when 23 other important trading nations are included, it can

Figure 10: Inflation–Adjusted Gold Prices
U.S. Compared with OECD

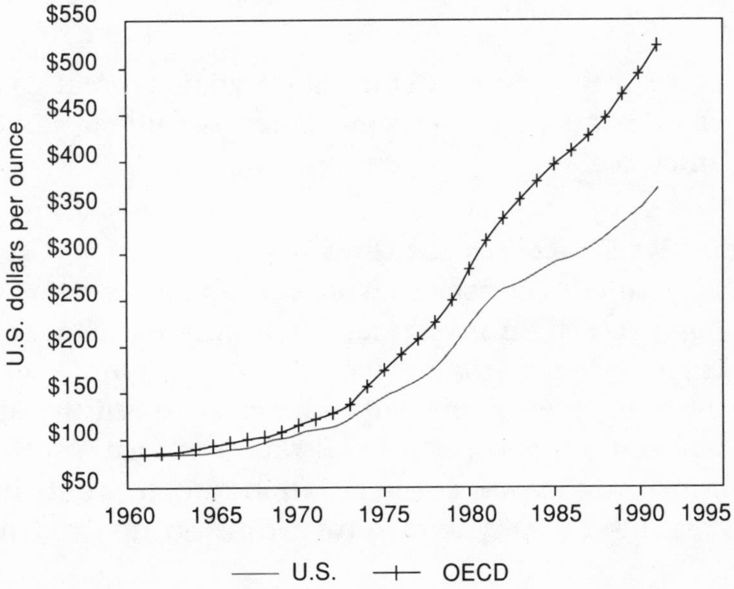

Figure 11: Real Value of Gold Assuming 2.5% Rate of Return Plus the Inflation Rate

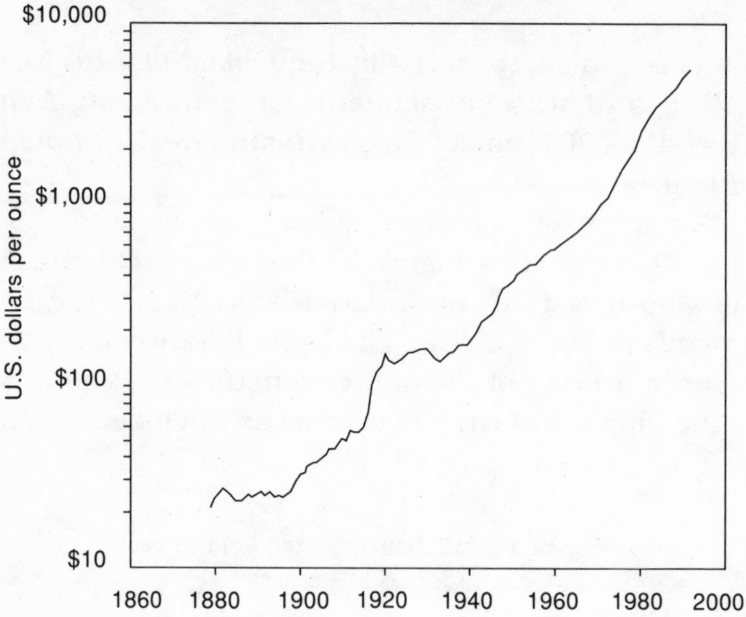

be seen that an OECD inflation-adjusted real gold value is about 40 percent higher in value at $525 an ounce.

A "Real" Return for Gold

Investment counselors who are capable of achieving a return on investment that only matches the current rate of inflation would be incapable of keeping their clients. Instead they must exceed the inflation rate, earning a "real rate of return" — the amount in excess of the inflation rate. It is only by earning a real rate of return that an investment manager protects the purchasing power of an investment portfolio.

Assuming a real rate of return of 2.5 percent per annum since 1879, the real value of gold bullion increases to $5,600 per ounce for the U.S. inflation rate experience. Using this adjusted real value, it can be argued that gold is truly undervalued at mid-1992 prices of around $340 per ounce. Our view, however, is that to expect gold to provide a real long-term rate of return may be overly ambitious. The lack of a real rate of return can be looked at as the cost of insurance or the price to be paid for gold's homogeneity, portability, and liquidity.

3. The Next 10 Years

In his 1990 book *The Age of Diminished Expectations*, Paul Krugman, professor of economics at the Massachusetts Institute of Technology and a former member of the staff of the President's Council of Economic Advisors, describes the most likely economic forecast for the United States in the next 10 years as "drift," or more of the same. We agree with Professor Krugman that the 1990s will in all likelihood resemble the last few years of the 1980s. Concerns about unemployment will be addressed as they have in the past 50 years: by pumping up the money supply, by administering lower interest rates, and by setting new, less restrictive banking regulations.

Somehow the U.S. administration will convince the entrepreneurs to come out from under their bushels. This decade will be the decade of new public equity issues, rather than of junk bonds. The economy will continue on a path of slow growth. There will be a modicum of increase in real incomes for a large part of the middle class, while the poor will probably see their real incomes contract slightly as a result of inflation, which will likely be at slightly higher levels overall than in the 1980s. Real economic growth should average better than 2 percent but less than 3 percent per annum. Inflation will likely drift around 6 to 7 percent without causing any real concern about the foreign-exchange trading range of the dollar.

Because of demographic patterns — the baby boomers are starting to retire — the growth of the workforce will probably slow relative to the 1980s. This will enable the U.S. governments to maintain unemployment rates at the late 1980s levels of about 5 percent.

Foreign investors will begin to convert their holdings of government debt to private equity. This conversion of loans to ownership will provide permanent capital in place of what currently appears as a massive foreign debt problem. Nonetheless, Middle Eastern petrodollars will continue to support the U.S. dollar.

The major risk to the U.S. dollar is the arrogance of the U.S. administration. The United States faces the technological superiority of Japan and an equally arrogant and fiscally conservative European Community dominated by Germany. To protect its own interests, the United States could start restrictive trade wars and perhaps devalue its currency. The most likely result, however, will be that the U.S. dollar will take second place in the world's economic horse race behind a unified Europe.

The hard-line gold bugs — those people who seem to believe that the only real money is gold — will look at this scenario and argue that the banks are bankrupt, that lowering interest rates is as useless as pushing on a string, that banks will not or cannot lend, and entrepreneurs will not play. According to the hard-line gold bug scenario, the result will be deflation. Their view is that declining interest rates will cause the dollar to fall and become unacceptable as the world's trading currency. Moreover, they predict that interest rates, which will be increased in an attempt to bolster the dollar, will further bankrupt the banking system. Consequently they can see only credit deflation — a flight from debt investments into gold.

The standard hard-landing case for the gold bugs was best described recently by Ian Lamont, of the London, England, office of Yorkton Securities Inc., in "The Coming Credit Deflation," an article in Yorkton's newsletter to clients, dated October 15, 1989:

In oiling the wheels and supplying reserves to the international banking system by running massive deficits, the U.S. dollar has become massively over supplied, and has little in the way of gold backing to support it. The first consequence of this was the consumer price inflation of the 1970s which resulted in a devaluation of the dollar against gold in 1972, and a general flight out of currencies into gold. This time it is even more serious as there has been asset price inflation on an unprecedented scale and this will require huge adjustments to correct. These adjustments are destined to cause enormous disruptions in the world as credit must be reduced and, just as happened in the early 1930s, we suspect that in the ensuing chaos and scramble for liquidity, countries will dump foreign exchange and seek out the only asset they can hold which is not someone else's liability, namely GOLD.

While we regard ourselves as gold bugs, we do not place too much credence in the regular "the sky is falling" scenario. The main reason to hold gold, as both Alan Greenspan and Ian Lamont know, is its ability to preserve wealth.

Gold's beauty, portability, homogeneity, and liquidity are what provide it with that attribute along with its ability to counter the politically acceptable and persistent tendency to inflation and, therefore, the depreciation of fixed-rate securities and currency.

Our scenario of "more of the same" for the 1990s will provide inflation rates at around 6 to 7 percent in the United States. OECD inflation rates will probably be slightly higher for the next 10 years but will tend to become closely aligned to U.S. levels as a result of a fiscally conservative, German-dominated European Economic Community. The problems of the U.S. budget and trade deficits will remain with us but will become comfortable if not acceptable to the world's banking community. The savings and loan and banking crises in the United

States will pass as massive amounts of foreign, domestic, and petrodollars are converted to equity ownership in a reorganized U.S. banking system that will consist of larger, better-financed entities. New banking rules and regulations will pave the way for this process. The system is vulnerable, but in the past it has proved to be very flexible and it should survive without a massive credit crunch.

Our view, while not the traditional hard-line gold bug forecast of catastrophe, has not kept us from remaining gold bugs. Almost any scenario that we paint leads to a most likely continuance of inflation worldwide. North American inflation will not be the runaway inflation of Brazil or Argentina. But as measured by OECD or U.S. standards it will be persistent, continuous, and, as always, depreciating to currencies.

4. Gold Will Almost Certainly Double in Price

Our best prediction, based on continuing inflation, is that the price of gold will increase on average by 7 percent a year to the year 2000. Figure 12 shows our predictions for the long-term gold value over the 1990s. This chart is an extension of the gold value derived from the 1879 gold price shown in figure 9. Although the chart is based on a 7 percent increase, we have included projections using 5 percent and 9 percent. Using 5 percent the price of gold would reach $572 by 2000; using 9 percent it would reach $831.

A 7 percent average annual increase would simply reflect the inflation rate. It does not allow for any real rate of return. Our predictions are based on our assumptions that the U.S. economy will continue to lose its dominant position relative to the other OECD countries, and that there will be a higher rate of inflation in the United States during

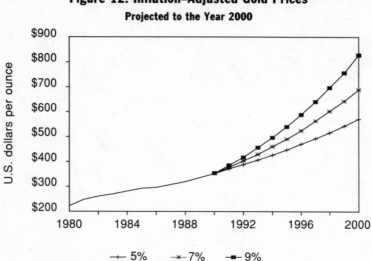

Figure 12: Inflation–Adjusted Gold Prices
Projected to the Year 2000

the 1990s. Nevertheless, events that are likely to occur over the next three to five years may lead to the doubling of the gold price much sooner. Moreover, it is possible that our target of $700 an ounce may be too conservative.

The events we expect during that time are:

- An increase in the demand for gold for jewelry. We base our expectation on growing world affluence as well as increased consumer demand in major economies stemming from the World Gold Council's promotion of high-caratage jewelry.
- A reduction in the supply of newly mined gold as many of the world's smaller gold mines run out of ore that can be economically produced and the larger mines encounter increased costs,

which in turn requires a higher cut-off point on the grades of ore that can be used (measured in fractions of ounces of gold per tonne of ore), and thus lower production.

- Currency unrest in Eastern Europe and the countries that make up the former Soviet Union, in the midst of an increase in economic well-being, should provide for an increase in the demand for gold.
- Speculative demand reaching a panic stage as fears about runaway inflation become more prevalent in some countries, such as Brazil and Argentina.
- A buying panic from major gold mining companies, which by and large have all adopted a policy that involves forward selling — selling gold for delivery some months, a year, or even several years in the future. This policy of selling gold forward is relatively new for the very conservative gold mining industry. Today it is considered aggressive not to have some of your future production hedged forward. Five years ago, few of the mining companies sold forward. (In a later chapter we study some of the intricate hedge programs that have been developed on Wall Street and that use unique gold derivative products.) For the most part, it means that gold mining companies are constantly "short" gold bullion to the market. In other words, they sold gold that they have borrowed and for which they must pay at some point either out of production or by purchasing gold in the market.

Since the company employees running the gold shorting book, and gold mining management in general, have no real long-term experience in these affairs, there is a high probability that panic buying will occur at the very time when prices move higher than the price at which the forward sales were made. That will be precisely the time that the market cannot or will not immediately be capable of providing the gold to cover the short position.

Several other potential developments could have a major influence on the price of gold. These include:

- Political turmoil in South Africa. Widespread unrest could easily close down many major mines. A peaceful solution to that country's problems could result in a sharp increase in production costs, which in turn would result in fewer mines being profitable.
- Political disruptions in the CIS. These would almost certainly reduce Russian gold production and would trigger panic buying of gold within and outside the countries of the former Soviet Union.
- A move by the European Economic Community to place the Ecu, the European currency unit, on a gold standard.
- A trade war with Japan, which would likely see Japan trying to reduce its U.S.-dollar foreign-exchange reserves by purchasing gold.

In addition to these specific events, other possible

or probable trends will affect the price of gold. These include continued mild inflation in the United States and other OECD nations; continuing trade and current-account deficits in the United States as well as the prevailing official arrogance about these problems; the vagaries of Eastern European economic experiments; the fall and rise of the countries of the former Soviet Union economically, politically, and militarily; a low level of real interest rates in the United States; no firm resolution to the Middle East situation; and a host of other problems that are as yet unknown and uncharted.

Moreover, the view that the United States would never opt for any type of gold standard because the Soviet Union and South Africa would be the major beneficiaries no longer holds. The dissolution of the Soviet empire and moves by South Africa to end apartheid clear the way for the United States to endorse greater use of gold in the international monetary system.

The convergence of any of these events could create a buying panic on the "money commodity." And the bear market in gold bullion that began after gold hit $850 an ounce in January 1980 could end with the price once again approaching its old high watermark.

It could all occur in the next three to five years.

II. Supply and Demand

TWICE EACH BUSINESS DAY VIRTUALLY ALL GOLD MINING company executives, jewelry manufacturers and retailers, investment dealers, senior bankers, investors, and speculators check their quotation terminals, look at newswires, or listen to the business news for the London gold "fixings." The fixings, quoted in U.S. dollars, indicate the prices at which large amounts of gold were traded at each fixing. Because the fixings reflect actual large sales, which may be measured in tonnes (one tonne equals 32,150 troy ounces), they are considered a true gauge of the gold market.

The fixings are established at N.M. Rothschild & Sons' London offices. Every weekday morning, just before 10:30 local time (and again in the afternoon), four men representing long-established gold dealers join the director of Rothschild's Bullion Division. Behind closed doors these five men repeat a ceremony that began in 1919 after wartime controls on gold sales were lifted and that has continued to the present, except for the period from 1939 to 1954, when the gold market was closed again because of wartime controls.

Although gold bullion can be bought and sold in most major centers, it is the London market where many of the world's largest orders to buy and sell gold are funneled by dealers. It is at the morning fix and again at the afternoon fix that these orders can be filled at a single price.

After the First World War, South African producers wanted to reestablish a market for their gold production. Their instructions to Rothschild's were to get the best price obtainable. Initially brokers placed their bids with Rothschild's by telephone. This system soon proved to be unworkable, however, and was quickly changed to a formal meeting at the Rothschild offices. Everyone attending would be able to buy and sell gold on equal terms with everyone else. One price would be quoted, the price at which all supplies could be absorbed in the market. In addition, certain standards of quality were set for "good delivery." To be suitable a bar must be at least 995 parts per thousand pure gold and must have been refined by one of about four dozen approved refiners around the world.

These conditions continue today. The meeting is held behind closed doors, and the volume of gold traded kept secret. Yet its method of deliberation is well known. Each of the five men is in contact with the trading room of his firm by telephone. His traders, in turn, are in contact with banks and major bullion dealers around the world. Each of the five has a small Union Jack on his desk. By saying "flag up" each dealer may halt deliberations while he confers with his trading room.

The chairman begins by suggesting an appropriate opening price based on prices in New York the previous evening or Hong Kong that morning. Each man relays the opening bid to his trading room, which has instructions from clients to buy or sell at specific prices or is online to clients who may make on-the-spot decisions. Only those orders that the dealer can't cross (match buy orders with sell orders) among his company's own clients are brought to the fix, and each dealer indicates whether he is a buyer or a seller. If a seller, he indicates how many 400-ounce bars he is offering.

If there are no sellers at the opening price, the bid is raised. If there are no buyers, the bid is lowered. Changes in prices will, of course, influence buyers and sellers, and orders do change. But when enough gold is offered at a specific price to match the buyers, the price is fixed. The price is immediately transmitted around the world and sets the tone of trading for the day.

The London gold market and the fixing are essential to the world gold market because only in London can buyers and sellers deal in quantity. London, however, is not the only major gold market. Zurich has been a major center since the late 1960s, channeling tons of production from South Africa and the former Soviet Union to world markets. Hong Kong, too, has become a major gold center. As well, the New York Commodity Exchange, or Comex, has become extremely important in the trading of what are called derivative products — futures and options contracts tied to gold.

The orders that are behind the London fix can originate virtually anywhere. A seller may be a major mining company or a central bank trying to raise cash to settle trade debts. A buyer could be a central bank building reserves or a jewelry manufacturer. But from whom the gold comes or to whom it is going is not relevant to the fix. What is relevant is the number of ounces being offered or bid and the price at which they will balance — simple supply and demand.

The law of supply and demand applies to gold just as it applies to every other good or service. If demand exceeds supply, the price goes higher. If supply exceeds demand, the price declines. The law of supply and demand is a fairly simple relationship, at least when applied to commodities such as wheat or coffee or copper. Yet it is extremely complex in the case of gold. Gold is both a commodity and a financial asset. As a commodity, its price will reflect demand from the jewelry manufacturing and electronics industries and supplies from mines and scrap, which includes gold jewelry, coins, and other objects melted for their gold content. As a financial asset, its price reflects gold purchases and sales of central banks which use gold as part of their exchange reserves to finance trade deficits. In addition, the price will reflect purchases and sales by investors, hedgers, and speculators. Indeed, these transactions are the key to substantial increases or decreases in the price of gold. A surge in investment demand will send prices soaring. However, a quick upward move in the price of gold will likely curb jewelry demand and at the same time encourage sales of old gold for its scrap value. Similarly, a jump in prices encourages mining companies to sell some or all of their anticipated production in the futures market. Conversely, heavy sales by investors will send prices tumbling, which in turn will affect how mining companies sell their gold.

Gold differs from most every other commodity traded in that it isn't consumed. Since virtually all the gold ever mined is owned by someone or some organization, such as a government treasury, there is always gold available to be borrowed, just as money can be borrowed from a bank. As a result, the tools economists use for predicting the prices of other commodities do not apply to gold, and their attempts to predict price movements of gold therefore often fail. For example, during the late 1970s gold prices jumped in concert with a jump in the price of oil. Some analysts developed models that tied the future price of gold to the price of oil. While the models seemed to work for a short time, investors who based their decisions on oil prices would have lost their shirts.

From time to time the gold market proves to be a volatile market because it is a "thin" market, which means it doesn't take much buying or selling to move the market substantially. To put this in perspective, total gold production in the Western world in 1991 was an estimated 55.7 million ounces, or $20 billion using a price of $360 an ounce. Compare that with the average daily trading value of shares on the New York Stock Exchange of $7 billion.

The market can also be influenced drastically by purchases and sales of gold futures, contracts that call for the delivery of specific amounts of gold at specified dates. Because these trade on an exchange and are very liquid, they are often the choice of speculators.

During the 1970s, gold prices rose because of demand from speculators and investors who sought high profits, or a means of protecting their assets against currency devaluation. In contrast, during the 1980s, gold performed poorly and many investors sold their holdings. But what's bad for investors is sometimes good for consumers, and lower gold prices helped send gold jewelry production and sales to record levels. This allowed the gold mining industry to expand, and mine production increased to record levels. The supply picture, however, will change by the mid-1990s.

5. The Supply of Gold

Traditionally, the gold industry has defined the supply of gold as the total of Western mine production, sales (including mine production and sales from reserves) from what used to be called the Communist countries, old gold scrap, and net official sales from central banks. These, of course, are all large components of gold supply. But the market is changing. Since the mid-1980s, what are called gold derivatives have had a major effect on supply. Gold derivatives include gold loans, forward sales, gold options, and spot deferreds, and together they contribute enough gold to be their own component of gold supply. Consequently our definition of gold supply includes a fifth component: net gold derivatives. Let's look at each of these sources in more detail.

Mine Production

Gold is found and mined in all parts of the world. South Africa is the largest producer, followed by the United States, the former Soviet Union, Australia, Canada, and Brazil.

Gold has been mined since the time of the ancient Egyptians, yet it was almost always in short supply until the 1700s. Until then gold was primarily the wealth of royalty and the richest of merchants, while silver and copper coins, which were tied to gold, were used for most transactions. Mining was primitive and non-mechanized. Countries could substantially increase their holdings of gold by stealing it, as Spain did in the 1500s. But on the whole the world gold supplies grew slowly. Some estimates put total cumulative world gold production from the time of the ancient Egyptians to 1850 at about 325 million ounces. Since 1850 world mine production has likely taken the total to well over 3 billion ounces.

The development of the gold standard as the basis of money came about because of substantial new gold supplies in the 1700s from Brazil and Russia. By the mid-1800s, Russia was the world's largest gold producer, with output of about 1.5 million ounces a year — about 60 percent of world production. (In comparison, world production excluding the former Soviet Union has been running at about 50 million ounces in recent years.) Gold production, however, entered a new era with major discoveries in the mid- and late 1800s, including the California gold rush and its counterparts in

Australia, the Klondike, and South Africa. It was these discoveries that provided the world with enough gold to go on the gold standard, which lasted until the First World War. Indeed, the amount of gold produced in the last half of the nineteenth century was equal to all the gold produced previously.

The modern gold mining industry began in 1887 with the development of the MacArthur-Forrest process for extracting gold from gold ore using a weak cyanide solution. This process allowed for recovery of about 96 percent of the gold from the ore. Gold mining got another boost in 1934 when the U.S. government raised the price of gold to $35 an ounce from $20.67. Annual world gold production (again excluding the former Soviet Union) doubled and reached a peak of 38.6 million ounces in 1940. But many of the best-producing mines were exhausted, and production declined to 24.3 million ounces in 1950.

Production rose in the 1950s to about 32 million ounces a year in 1959 and reached a plateau above 38 million ounces a year through most of the 1960s and early 1970s before declining to under 32 million ounces. Between 1980 and 1990 annual production in non-Communist countries rose about 80 percent, from about 31 million ounces to 55.7 million ounces.

During the 1980s, major shifts in production took place, with South African production declining and North American production rising. In 1980, South Africa was responsible for 70 percent of non-Communist world gold production. For 1990 South Af-

rica's share was about 35 percent. In 1980 North
America accounted for about 8.5 percent of non-
Communist world gold production; in 1990 it accounted for an estimated 27 percent. This trend
will continue, and by 1995 South African production will be only marginally higher than the North
American level.

Production and Exploration Decisions
The long-lasting bear market in the gold price is
beginning to have its effect on production and exploration decisions. The decisions that put some
mines in production during the late 1980s were
made in the early 1980s, when gold prices were
$500 an ounce or higher. Today, only a handful of
mining properties around the world are awaiting
production decisions. Moreover, more and more
companies have been focusing their exploration ac-
tivities on metals other than gold. While they believe gold prices will move higher, they see mining
other metals as a better use of capital.

Growth depends on exploration levels, ability to
bring mines into production, and technological developments. High exploration levels are unlikely in
Canada and the United States so long as the price
of gold is below $400 an ounce. In recent years the
cash cost of production of a typical North American
gold mine was about $240 an ounce. To that can
be added a factor of $50 for capital expenditures
and another $50 for exploration costs. As well, a
company would allocate another $10 to cover the
actual cost of capital over the life of a mine. These

additions raise the total cost to about $340 an ounce, leaving as a real operating margin the difference between that figure and the current gold price. Given the risks in the gold mining business, margins have been insufficient, on average, to justify new production. In addition, production costs continue to face inflationary pressures. These costs exclude any allocations for exploration and capital expenditures, and they suggest that the North American gold mining industry is essentially operating at break-even or loss levels. The gold mining industry cannot attract large amounts of speculative capital to finance exploration because of the low price of gold, high real interest rates, and shrinking cash flows. Shrinking cash flows mean major companies do not have the funds necessary for large-scale company-sponsored exploration programs. Without a surge in gold prices, many marginal mines will continue to lose cash. The result will be additional closures.

If gold prices were to surge higher, some marginal mines would likely reopen. Yet this would have only a small influence on the volume of gold produced around the world over the next several years. This is because about 85 percent of the Western world's mines are profitable, based on cash costs, with the price of gold at $350. Higher prices would eventually lead to more exploration and mine development, which would be reflected in world production figures in the future.

However, should the price of gold decline to, say, to $300 an ounce, only 72 percent of production would be economic, and many mines would have to close. At $200 an ounce only 30 percent of production would be economic. Consequently, the price of gold appears to have a floor in the $300 to $350 range. Any decline below that range would almost certainly result in mines closing and a substantial cut in world gold production, which in turn would send prices higher again.

It therefore seems likely that world production will decline by the mid-1990s no matter what happens to gold prices because new mines will not be developed in time to replace those whose reserves are exhausted. Indeed, there are few new mines scheduled to open over the next few years or awaiting feasibility studies and environmental impact assessments. With the exception of Eskay Creek in British Columbia and a few others, the properties scheduled for development have relatively low grades and will likely require higher gold prices for positive production decisions. Furthermore, political risks continue to affect development timetables of mines outside North America.

South Africa

While South Africa is still the world production leader, its mine production has declined from 21.7 million ounces in 1980 to an estimated 19.5 million ounces in 1990. Production and margins have declined for several reasons. First, inflation has been considerably higher in recent years than in most of the Western world. Consequently, the mining industry's costs have risen at a much higher pace than has the price of gold. Second, the mining industry has faced and will continue to face large wage increases, particularly as the political situation evolves and apartheid is broken down. Third, gold has become much less important to the South African economy than it once was. Whereas at one time the South African government would devalue the rand to protect the mining industry's margins, it can no longer afford to sacrifice the value of its currency for the benefit of the gold industry. Consequently, the industry's profit margins have been so eroded that industry analysts estimate that a substantial portion of South African gold is produced at a loss.

Why, one might ask, hasn't South Africa shut down its unprofitable production? The answer lies in the fact that South Africa's deposits are deep and narrow, and so the costs of mothballing uneconomic mines would be prohibitive. Indeed, the capital costs of closing then reopening a mine more than one mile deep would be enormous. Even so, South Africa has embarked on a major cost-cutting program, which has slowed the escalation of costs.

In addition, lower-grade stopes — working areas in mines — are being closed and production is being shifted to higher-grade areas. While these moves should help mining profitability over the short term, the quality of the remaining reserves will deteriorate.

With inflation continuing at double-digit levels and production costs at some mines already above the price of gold, it is hard to imagine that South

African production will not continue to decline. A five-year forecast published by the World Gold Council predicts that annual production will decline by 11 percent to 1995. While we feel that the potential production drop could in fact be much more dramatic, we have used their estimates for our forecast.

North America

As noted previously, North American annual production grew tremendously over the 1980s, increasing almost sixfold, from less than 3 million ounces in 1980 to about 14.8 million ounces in 1991. Production in 1992 will almost certainly be higher as a result of the final stages of development of the more than 20-million-ounce Goldstrike Mine of American Barrick. This mine should produce gold at an annual rate of 1 million ounces by 1992. In Canada, the Eskay Creek deposit should be producing 250,000 ounces of gold by 1995.

Yet even with these new mines, North American production will likely peak in 1992. Deposits such as the Colomac Mine of Northwest Gold have closed because of lack of financing. A partial list of other mines whose production life may be limited include the Arthur White Mine of Dickenson because of its high costs; the Fortitude Mine of Battle Mountain because of depleted reserves; Placer Dome's Detour Lake, Sigma, and Kiena mines because of high costs; and Corona's Nickel Plate Mine, also because of high costs. A higher gold price may prolong the life of some of these mines.

In addition, much of the increase in North American production during the 1980s came from discoveries in Nevada that are exploited using heap-leach technologies. (These low-grade deposits in relatively dry areas are put into production using open-pit mining. Ore is piled on a protective leach pad and a cyanide solution allowed to percolate through the ore. The solution leaches out the gold for processing.) But many of the newer mines have short lives. In the absence of new technologies to exploit these ore bodies, production will almost certainly decline. And even if new technologies are developed, it will be several years before the industry enjoys the benefits.

The expansion of production will also be limited by environmental concerns. All indications are that the 1990s will be the decade of the environmental movement. Complying with new regulations means higher costs, delays, and even the elimination of mining from some areas. In some cases, compliance is a matter of meeting new, tougher regulations that limit what can be discharged into the environment. These changes raise production costs and could lead to the closing of marginal mines.

Environmental impact statements, which are comprehensive reports on how mining each new deposit affects the surrounding environment, are becoming a standard procedure for mining companies considering mine expansion or development. These statements and public hearings can delay production decisions by years or result in an area being closed to mining. For example, a two-year moratorium on a new large-scale open-pit mine in South Dakota resulted from the conflict between those people who want the economic benefits of mining and those who see their recreational areas threatened by mine development. The moratorium was put into place by the mining industry because of concern that in the absence of a moratorium it would face legislation that might permanently ban mine expansion in that area. In addition, complying with local, regional, and federal rules can cause delays and add to costs. In future years the mining industry will likely see pressure for even higher royalties to pay for environmental programs and to finance reclamation or restoration of properties to pre-mining conditions.

The net result of the increased environmental awareness will be that mines will take longer to build and their capital costs will be higher. In other words, the economics of developing new deposits are getting more difficult, even without a decrease in the price of gold.

Of course, no ore bodies can be found without exploration. And with gold prices relatively low, few companies can justify large-scale exploration programs. Moreover, there is little incentive for individual investors and speculators to provide risk capital for exploration in the absence of a buoyant market for shares of junior gold exploration companies. It can be as much as a decade between the time a property is explored and the time a mine goes into production. The rising prices of the late 1970s and expectations that prices would be high in the

1980s encouraged companies to increase their exploration budgets for the search of gold. Many production decisions were made on the basis of price projections that have proved to be incorrect.

In addition to the high gold prices in the 1980s, North America's desire to rid itself of South African gold equities made raising equity capital for gold mining a fairly easy venture. In Canada, the Vancouver Stock Exchange played a major speculative role in raising significant amounts of risk capital, some of which found mines.

Much of the exploration in Canada between 1983 and 1990 was financed by tax assistance through what are called flow-through limited partnerships. As in many other countries, the Canadian government has tax incentive programs to encourage exploration and resource development. But many companies, especially the smaller ones, didn't have any taxable profits against which to take these deductions. Flow-through limited partnerships allowed certain exploration and other deductions to flow through from the companies receiving the funds to the investors supplying the funds. The program also included some cash grants. So the investor received shares in the resource companies, some cash grants, and deductions that could be applied against other taxable income. The effect was to allow the investor who put up the risk capital to use tax assistance to reduce risk.

The flow-through concept worked well. Investors benefited from high returns and the reduction of risk; large and small mining companies benefited from the availability of exploration funds. Flow-through funds resurrected Canada's exploration industry and provided thousands of jobs. The economy benefited from the mines that were developed, and government benefited from the tax dollars generated on income and from the unemployment benefits it didn't have to pay. However, in an attempt to trim its budget deficit, the Canadian government changed the rules, effectively ending flow-through financings as a means of raising exploration capital in Canada.

The addition of a 5 percent net profits tax in Nevada has cut exploration in that state as well. Our production estimates for North America are slightly lower than the World Gold Council's estimates.

Australia and Papua New Guinea
Australian gold production increased more than fourteenfold during the 1980s. As is the case in Nevada, much of this growth has been with short-life deposits that could be exploited using heap-leach technologies. Australian production of 7.8 million ounces during 1990 was a record and was largely the result of high grading or the exploitation of the highest-grade ores in order to beat the imposition of taxation effective in 1991. Australian production should peak by the middle of the decade, then decline. We are more conservative in our estimate than the World Gold Council.

Papua New Guinea has substantial gold deposits. The key question currently is whether the giant 44-million-ounce Lihir Island deposit owned by RTZ and New Guinea Mining will be put into production soon. In early 1992, RTZ was claiming that the potential return was too low to justify development. New Guinea Mining, on the other hand, was claiming that the return is adequate for development. While it is likely this deposit will be developed, the time frame will almost certainly be longer than previously expected, and gold will not be available for at least several years.

Latin America
Many Latin American countries suffered economically during the 1980s, and they are trying to encourage new investment. Indeed, more and more North American and European companies are allocating funds for exploration and development in Brazil, Chile, Venezuela, Guyana, and Mexico. As a group these countries do not produce a lot of gold. Much of Brazil's gold is produced by 40,000 *garimpeiros*, who work small claims and sell their production for cash. Latin America has the potential for growth as a gold producer during the 1990s. The magnitude of this growth depends largely on the area's social and political developments. While our estimates are higher than the World Gold Council's, we feel that ours may be conservative.

Sales from Former Soviet Union and Other
Eastern Bloc countries
Trying to estimate gold sales and production by former Soviet Union and other Eastern bloc countries is a mug's game. In the past, gold sales and pro-

duction figures were considered state secrets. Even with the moves away from communism to various forms of free-market economies and levels of democracy, old traditions have not changed quickly, and it may be several years before accurate reserve, production, and sales figures become available, if they do at all, unless the former members of the Soviet Union and other Eastern bloc countries decide to back their currencies or debt with gold.

Gold Fields Mineral Services estimated in 1991 that the Soviet Union produces about 9.6 million ounces of gold a year. That figure would make it the world's second-largest gold producer, after South Africa. However, subsequent to Gold Fields's report the world has learned much about Soviet production and reserves. Key was the announcement just before the break-up of the Soviet Union that gold reserves were only 8 million ounces, far below the 48 million to 65 million ounces many analysts expected. It seems likely, therefore, that the Soviets probably sold larger amounts of gold from reserves than previously thought and, consequently, drove prices lower than they would otherwise be. It is also likely that the production of the former Soviet Union is probably considerably less than 9.6 million ounces a year. We therefore conclude that the countries that were part of the Soviet Union will not continue to be the major sellers of gold they were, simply because they have run out of gold to sell. Production levels almost certainly reflect inefficient operations, employee smuggling, and general national uncertainty. While this does not bode well for Russia, it should bode well for gold.

An important point about Russian production is that about 70 percent is from placer mines (where gold is found mixed loosely with gravel and is extracted using fairly unsophisticated methods) while only about 30 percent of reserves are placer reserves. Russia will therefore need substantial capital before it can bring its other reserves into production efficiently. Even if it were able to attract capital and Western technical expertise quickly, it would be many years before production could begin to increase.

China is a smaller yet significant source of gold, producing about 2.7 million to 3.2 million ounces annually. China, however, probably uses all the gold it produces and has been an importer of foreign gold.

Gold Fields Mineral Services has estimated that in the late 1980s, the Soviet Union and other Eastern bloc countries sold between 2.7 million and 12.9 million ounces of gold. Industry estimates placed 1990 sales at between 11.3 million ounces and 12.9 million ounces. Given the disclosure in late 1991 of reserve levels of the former Soviet Union, the industry has generally cut its estimates and expectations of Eastern bloc production for the remainder of the decade.

While our numbers differ slightly from the estimates of the World Gold Council, our projected trends are similar. World gold production will probably rise moderately from 55.7 million ounces in

1990 to 58.1 million ounces in 1992. Annual world production will likely begin to decline after 1992, falling back to 1990's production level by the middle of the 1990s. What is key is that world gold production, which had a 6 percent average annual growth rate through the 1980s, is slowing and will soon turn negative.

Table 1 outlines world mine production history as well as our production forecast to 1995, along with the World Gold Council's forecast for comparison.

Old Gold Scrap
While recycling may seem a development of the 1980s and 1990s, recycling of gold is as old as gold fabrication itself. And as with every recyclable commodity, the availability of gold scrap is a reflection of the price of gold and the conditions of a local economy. If the price of gold moves higher, the availability of scrap gold increases, as it did in 1980 and 1986. Conversely, when the price is perceived to be low, the volume of scrap sold into the marketplace declines. In some soft-currency economies (in which government sets artificial values on a country's currency), where people are prohibited from owning gold in an investment form and high-carat jewelry is purchased for investment purposes, scrap sales may increase independently of the price of gold.

Sources of scrap include jewelry, industrial products such as recycled computer parts, and bullion coins. Scrap supply figures may have become dis-

Table 1: Mine Production (millions of ounces)

	1980	1981	1982	1983	1984	1985	1986	1987	1988	1989	1990	1991	1992	1993	1994	1995
														Goodman & Company forecast		
South Africa	21.70	21.14	21.36	21.85	21.97	21.60	20.58	19.52	19.97	19.55	19.39	19.32	19.23	18.97	18.65	18.16
United States	0.98	1.41	1.46	2.01	2.12	2.56	3.80	4.98	6.46	8.33	9.71	9.65	10.29	10.22	10.13	10.06
Canada	1.66	1.70	2.14	2.35	2.76	2.89	3.40	3.75	4.33	5.09	5.27	5.69	5.47	5.47	5.47	5.40
Australia	0.55	0.59	0.87	0.98	1.26	1.88	2.41	3.56	5.05	6.33	7.78	7.52	7.23	6.75	6.43	6.11
Papua New Guinea	0.46	0.55	0.57	0.59	0.60	1.01	1.16	1.09	1.18	1.08	1.13	1.95	2.25	2.41	2.48	2.57
Latin America	2.94	3.34	3.43	4.59	4.90	5.68	5.75	6.51	7.43	7.33	7.39	6.75	6.91	7.26	7.62	7.88
Other	2.63	2.92	3.33	3.51	3.88	4.12	4.56	5.07	5.44	5.42	5.62	6.56	6.75	6.91	6.91	7.07
Total	30.92	31.67	33.15	35.89	37.50	39.73	41.66	44.47	49.85	53.14	56.29	57.44	58.13	57.99	57.68	57.26
World Gold Council forecast													57.16	56.07	55.65	54.94

* Figures have been rounded.
Source: Gold Fields Mineral Services, Goodman & Company

torted in recent years by the wide-scale melting of South African Krugerrands in Europe and North America as investors avoided these coins because of South Africa's politics and bought instead Canadian Maple Leaf and other bullion coins. As well, many investors who were disappointed with the performance of gold sold their gold coins, many of which were melted as scrap. For forecasting purposes we are assuming that scrap availability will be about 10.5 million ounces of gold per year.

Net Official Sales from Central Banks

The buying and selling of gold by the "official sector" — that is, central banks and government investment institutions — has a major influence on gold prices. Governments hold gold as a reserve against foreign trade obligations. Unlike foreign exchange reserves, which can be devalued by the issuing government, gold is not an obligation of any government. There is also a limited amount. Of the 100 000 tonnes of gold mined over the past 5,000 years, central banks own about one-third. Holding gold reserves gives a nation flexibility in its international dealings. A country needing dollars to meet its immediate obligations could borrow the money, using its gold reserves as security. This would generally not require a physical movement of gold as it is quite common for countries to keep their gold with the Federal Reserve Bank of New York or the Bank of England.

Official world gold holdings in central banks are about 29 500 tonnes, or almost 950 million ounces.

As well, the International Monetary Fund and similar institutions hold an additional 6100 tonnes. Gold as a percentage of total reserves against foreign trade obligations was about 33 percent in 1989, at an average price of $381 an ounce. In 1981, when the average price of gold was $460, it was 57 percent of total reserves. The percentage of a country's reserves that are held as gold varies from country to country. Japan has only about 11 percent of its reserves in gold; Switzerland has about 56 percent; the United States has 95 percent.

However, because the U.S. dollar is the world's reserve currency, the United States' foreign-exchange needs are minor. It keeps some foreign currencies as reserves in case they are needed to help stabilize the dollar in currency markets.

It is very difficult if not impossible to predict official sales or purchases. While some analysts speculate that central banks have been large sellers over the years, Gold Fields Mineral Services' figures indicate that net official sales were negative, or, in fact, purchases, during the period from 1980 to 1989 and totaled 24.8 million ounces.

What will happen in the future is anyone's guess. There is always the possibility that central banks will sell some of their gold — this might occur if the price surged and investors moved from paper assets to gold. Conversely, central banks might become widespread buyers if they believed that increasing gold reserves would increase confidence in their currencies. We estimate that central banks sold 3 million ounces of gold in 1991. For 1992 and subsequent years we are estimating annual sales of about 2 million ounces.

Policies toward holding gold vary from country to country. Canada, for example, has been reducing its gold holdings over the past decade and sold about 1.8 million ounces in 1991 and an additional half-million ounces in the first two months of 1992. In contrast, Taiwan has been building its gold reserves, as did many oil-producing nations when oil prices surged in the 1970s. Indeed, governments were the major purchasers of gold in the period after the Second World War to the mid-1960s.

Most countries buy or sell gold only to adjust their reserves. However, circumstances can change policies dramatically. For example, Iran and Iraq were likely major sellers of gold during the years they fought each other. Indeed, Iraq was reported to have seized Kuwait's gold reserves during its invasion in 1990 and rumors of sales of this gold contributed to a lower gold price during much of the year. As well, the former Soviet Union, as noted earlier, was traditionally a major seller of gold to finance its foreign currency needs.

The rebuilding of the Eastern European economy will require much capital, and it is not out of the question that some gold will be sold. However, countries such as Poland, Hungary, and Romania have little gold — less than 2 million ounces collectively.

Net Gold Derivatives
Since the mid-1980s mining companies have been selling future production into the market through

gold loans, forward sales, and spot deferreds. Mining companies use these tactics to protect themselves against a decline in the price of gold and to lock in what may prove to be a premium price for gold. This is called "hedging." Hedging tactics reduce risk of falling prices. However, they also limit future profits by putting a ceiling on the price that the mining company will receive for its gold.

Gold loans work like this: A gold mining company that needs capital, say, to put a mine into production, borrows gold rather than cash from a bank. It agrees to repay the loan in gold. It also agrees to pay the interest in gold at a rate of 2 percent — far below what it would pay if it borrowed cash. The mining company then sells the gold it has just borrowed and uses the proceeds to pay for its project. Later, the mining company takes the gold it produces from its mines and, instead of selling it, repays its loan to the bank in gold.

Gold loans have had the effect of increasing the supply of gold to the marketplace since the late 1980s. This increased supply is one of the reasons gold prices did not move higher during the 1980s.

Even though the gold sold is not yet mined at the time the sale is made, the effect on supply is immediate because an offsetting amount of gold is borrowed, generally from a central bank, and sold into the market. Importantly, sales of future production should be looked at in the context of reducing future supplies to the market because the gold loan must be replaced from the mine's production.

There are a number of variations of the gold loan. Forward sales and spot deferreds are contracts requiring the delivery of gold at a specified future date at a price based on the spot price — the price at which gold is trading for immediate delivery at the time the contract is made plus a premium to the market called the "contango." The contango is based on prevailing interest rates. In effect a dealer leases gold from a central bank and sells the gold at the spot price, then invests the money in, say, treasury bills to cover the contango. The dealer who has bought the forward-sales contract intends to replace the gold borrowed with the gold he or she will receive from the producer. The dealer's profit is the fee he or she receives from the mining company.

In effect gold loans, forward sales, and spot deferreds are the equivalent of short sales — selling borrowed gold with the intention of repaying the loan out of gold yet to be mined. They put pressure on gold prices because they have the effect of increasing supply. But eventually, as the loans are repaid and as more and more of the world's production goes into unwinding these contracts rather than being sold into the marketplace, they will push gold prices higher.

Hedging by gold producers, which generally have very conservative management, is a recent development. In 1982, Australian producers became the first to use gold loans to finance mine development. North American producers followed in the mid-1980s. South African producers have started hedging programs more recently.

Few senior mining executives fully understand

hedging techniques or appreciate the risks involved. They first instituted hedging as a way to lessen the effect of widely fluctuating gold prices on their operations. And because hedging has tended to improve cash flow, companies that had not used hedging techniques found themselves adopting the technique in order to be competitive. However, the hedging function is often the responsibility of junior employees who, through lack of experience, fail to realize the effect hedging may have on a company's cash flow should the price of gold surge. Any hedging operation has a cost. And while it places a floor on the price to be received for future production, it also places a ceiling on the price to be received down the road. Consequently, companies that use hedging extensively may not benefit fully from increases in the price of gold. This is an important consideration for analysts and investors in determining the leverage, or effect, that rising gold prices would have on the value of gold producers' shares. A $100-an-ounce increase in the price of gold would have a lot more leverage on the share price of a company that has sold forward none of its production than on that of a company that has sold, say, 50 percent or more of its production.

Moreover, gold hedging through forward sales, spot deferred sales, and gold loans affects the amount of gold that is supplied to the market by producers. Whereas analysts have traditionally used gold production as the key figure in making supply estimates, they now have to factor in the volume of production hedged.

The amount of gold production hedged is significant. Gold Fields estimates that the total amount of gold production hedged is approximately 56 percent of one year's world production. (North American and Australian producers have been hedging in excess of 10 percent of their reserves.) The effect of hedging is cumulative, and at the end of 1990 about 20 million ounces of future production had been hedged.

Hedging programs have a definite influence on the price of bullion. For example, when the United States and its allies commenced their bombing of Iraq and Kuwait on January 16, 1991, the price of gold, which had been rising, in anticipation of war, from about $390, moved above $400. Some producers took advantage of the jump to sell forward, in effect putting a cap on the market. Supply very quickly exceeded demand, and the price of a gold futures contract on the Comex for February delivery plunged the following day by about $30 an ounce to $360. Part of the decline was undoubtedly the result of expectations that the war would be short-lived. But it also reflected the sales by at least several mining companies at the same time. An isolated incident, perhaps, but one that demonstrates how derivatives influence the market.

In early 1992, forward selling appeared to have placed a short-term ceiling on the price of gold at $370 an ounce. When gold approached this price, producers increased their forward selling, putting a cap on the price. Conversely, they withdrew from the market when the price moved lower, approaching $350 an ounce. The $350-an-ounce price was considered the floor because, below that price, many South African mines operate at a loss. In effect, hedging stabilizes the price of gold within a narrow range.

The use of hedging is likely to increase in the near term, particularly by South African producers, who are facing rising costs as well as declining ore grades and who have made limited use of hedging. Moreover, South Africa is unlikely to reintroduce its policy of devaluing the rand to offset falling gold prices. In fact, the South African Reserve Bank has been encouraging producers to use hedging.

Limits to Hedging
There are limits to how much of a producer's future production and reserves can be hedged. At some point, gold previously sold using hedging techniques must be delivered, in effect reducing supplies of new gold from producers to the market and removing the ceiling from the marketplace.

Take the case of spot deferred sales, a popular method of hedging by gold mining companies. Spot deferred sales between a producer and a major gold dealer or bank involve selling gold for future delivery at a price that reflects the contango — similar to forward sales. However, with a spot deferred sale, the delivery date and price are only tentative. If on the tentative delivery date, the previously agreed-upon spot deferred delivery price is more than the spot or market price, the producer would deliver gold against the spot deferred contract and receive the proceeds as stipulated in the contract. If, however, the spot deferred price is less than the spot price, the producer will sell its gold in the spot market and receive the spot price, and roll its spot deferred contract forward, setting another tentative delivery date with a new, higher price based on the contango.

In a rising market, spot deferred contracts could be deferred several times. The contract price in such a case would be the spot price of the initial transaction plus the total of the contangos from each deferral.

However, spot deferred contracts cannot be rolled over indefinitely. Depending on the terms of the contract, the dealer with whom the producer has contracted may decide not to allow the rollover of the spot deferred contract. This would happen if the price of gold sharply increased so that the spot price was substantially higher than the spot deferred price. In effect, the producer is "short" the market, or, in other words, owes gold it does not have and must deliver out of production or by buying an offsetting amount in the market. And if the price of gold starts to rise, producers who have used spot deferreds could find themselves forced into the market to buy gold to cover their positions. Their buying would, in turn, push prices even higher.

The Effect of Forward Selling on Spot Price
The forward sale of gold on an ongoing basis by mining companies influences the spot price. Say a

gold mining company decides to hedge against a possible decline in the price of gold by selling 100,000 ounces forward to a gold dealer. That dealer will likely offset his risk by selling an equivalent amount of gold in the spot market or futures market. The portion sold in the spot market will have a short-term effect on the price.

Alternatively, that gold mining company could use the options market to hedge against a decline. Options are contracts that give the holder the right to buy, in the case of call options, or sell, in the case of put options, a specified amount of gold up to a specific date at a set price. For example, a company could buy out-of-the-money put options covering 100,000 ounces. The term "out-of-the-money" means that the price at which the option would be triggered — the strike price — is below the market price. The risk, then, for the mining company, should the price decline, is limited to the difference between current market and the strike price of the options. On the other side of the transaction, the "writer," or the seller of the put options, now has a potential obligation to buy 100,000 ounces should the price of gold decline. If the price of gold starts declining, the writer, who is probably a gold dealer, would start selling gold in the market in anticipation of replacing the gold sold with gold that will be acquired when the put options are exercised. In effect, the dealer is hedging his obligation. (Dealers use a complicated mechanism called the "delta hedge" to measure how much gold they must buy or sell to offset their risk. The name reflects the triangular shape of the graph that shows the profit and loss potential from granting options.)

It is virtually impossible to tell precisely how much influence derivative products have on the spot price. While volumes of options and futures traded on exchanges are public knowledge and obtainable by reading any major business paper, a major of total trading consists of transactions between principals. Trades in this so-called over-the-counter market are private transactions and are not disclosed. Moreover, over-the-counter options don't have standard expiry dates, as do exchange options. So their influence is not measurable in the same way that the influence of expiry dates of exchange-traded options are measurable.

Over-the-counter options differ from exchange-traded options in a number of ways in addition to expiry dates. These differences reflect the specific needs of the parties involved. Some OTC options are termed "American." These can be exercised any time up to the expiry date. Others are termed "European" and can be exercised only on the expiry date. Conventional options are based on the price of gold at some specific date in the future. Average price options, or APOs, are based on the average price of gold over an agreed-upon period, which can be any period over the life of the option, usually weeks or even months. Some mining companies prefer using APOs because they are a more realistic reflection of the market and because they are less expensive since average prices are less volatile than spot prices.

A mining company's hedging program would reflect its expectations of the future price of gold as well as its specific needs for cash. A company with high cash costs per ounce would likely want more price insurance than would a company with significantly lower cash costs, that enable it to afford more price risk. There is, of course, a trade-off. The more certainty a mining company wants, the greater its costs in terms of premiums paid.

6. The Demand for Gold

The demand for gold has traditionally come from jewelry, electronics, dentistry, official and commemorative coins, investment by individuals, and as official reserves by central banks.

Jewelry

Gold has been used for jewelry and decorative objects for thousands of years. In its earliest form gold jewelry probably consisted of a nugget on a leather thong or in a crudely hammered shape. Jewelry-making was a skilled art by the time of the pharaohs 5,000 years ago. Almost certainly its use in ancient times was restricted to the powerful, wealthy, and privileged for their personal adornment, as signals of their station and for use in their religious rituals. Of course, it also signified wealth — and, more importantly, wealth that was portable.

Gold was truly a scarce commodity until the eighteenth century. In modern times, ownership of gold jewelry has become widespread, and in 1990 a record amount of gold was used in manufacturing jewelry — 1986 tonnes, or 64 million ounces — more than that year's world mining production (excluding that of the former Soviet Union). Indeed, jewelry has been the major market for gold over the past decade. Major growth markets during the 1980s included Europe and Japan as well as the developing countries. As the economies of Russia and the other countries that formerly were part of the Soviet Union, and of Eastern Europe are rebuilt and as the economies of China and Latin America expand, large markets for gold jewelry will develop. Gold jewelry and items made from gold are financial assets in countries where ownership of gold bullion is prohibited. Take, for example, the former Soviet Union. Before the dissolution of that empire there were reports indicating rising demand for gold jewelry despite a surge in prices as individuals tried to convert their rubles, which were losing value in a market that had few consumer goods, into a real asset.

Gold is a soft metal and is usually mixed with other metals to make it harder. Pure gold, or as pure as gold can be refined, is 24 carat or .999 fineness. Jewelry with 75 percent gold content — .750 fineness — is 18-carat gold, while 14-carat is 58.3 percent gold, or .583 fineness. The minimum legal standard for gold jewelry in the United States is 10 carat, or .416 fineness. Minimum caratage in Canada and England is 9 carat, while France and Italy require 18 carat. Turkey and other Eastern countries generally work with 22-carat gold.

Most gold jewelry produced — about two-thirds — is 14 carat, while about 10 percent is 18 carat or higher. Almost all the remainder is 10 carat. A necklace made of 10-carat gold would be substantially less expensive than a necklace of 18-carat gold. Consequently, these ratios tend to change with the price of gold.

Jewelry is manufactured around the world. Italy has historically been the largest fabricator, accounting for about 20 percent of gold used in jewelry in 1991, followed by Japan, 13 percent; India, 11 percent; the United States, and Taiwan, 6 percent; and Saudi Arabia, Turkey and Thailand. Southeast Asia has also become a major manufacturing center in recent years.

Demand for jewelry, however, is generally dependent on price. Between 1978 and 1980, as the price of gold surged from less than $200 an ounce to more than $700 an ounce, jewelry production declined from more than 51 million ounces to about 32 million ounces. Conversely, Japan has become a major market for its own gold jewelry as well as that it imports. Although increasing affluence is behind much of the demand, demand also reflects a declining price for gold in yen. Between 1983 and 1989 the price of an ounce of gold in yen fell by more than half.

Jewelry prices in a specific market will also reflect any luxury taxes. These, in turn, affect demand. Moreover, sales are very sensitive to consumer confidence. The purchase of jewelry is easily postponed by consumers worried about economic recession. As the North American economy headed into recession in the fall of 1990, continuing a trend that began the previous year, jewelry sales declined. In Japan, jewelry sales suffered in 1990 as a result of a major decline in the stock market, which wiped out billions of dollars of wealth.

Jewelry, of course, can be a financial asset. But it may a poor one because the retail price of an object may far exceed the value of its gold content. In some parts of the world, however, gold jewelry is considered an investment. Indeed, in some developing countries, particularly those where owning gold bars is prohibited, high-carat gold items — 22 carat, or 916 parts per thousand — are looked at as investments, and demand increases during times of prosperity as excess disposable income is used to purchase jewelry. Because the labor content is negligible relative to the gold value, such jewelry is effectively an investment rather than an ornament.

The demand for jewelry, while sensitive to price and general economic conditions, is likely to grow over the coming decade because of growing affluence, particularly in the Far East. Moreover, there will probably be a move toward higher-caratage jewelry, from 10 carat and 14 carat.

The World Gold Council, an association sponsored by gold mining companies, was established to increase demand for gold. Its promotional efforts have been aimed at increasing jewelry demand, and its promotional campaigns have been successful. In effect, the World Gold Council plans to do for gold what the De Beers selling group did for diamonds.

In addition to its use in carat jewelry, about 19 million ounces a year are used as gold plating, gold fill, and rolled gold in manufacturing costume jewelry, plumbing fixtures, eyeglass frames, pen and pencil sets, china, and glassware. Demand from this sector has been fairly steady over the past decade. Growth is likely to be modest, since technologies that require less gold to be used in electroplating have been recently developed.

Electronics
Gold is used in the electronics industry because of its electrical conductivity, its ability to be easily worked, and its virtual immunity to oxidization. Its major use is in plating of switch contacts and connectors and in semiconductors. In the early 1980s, when prices skyrocketed, gold lost market share to alloys and other metals. However, it has maintained its dominance in the manufacture of connectors used in the defense, business, and telecommunications markets. About 4.4 million ounces of gold were used in electronics in 1991. This market will likely keep step with the growth of the electronics industry.

Dentistry
Gold has been used in dentistry for thousands of

years and, in fact, few materials are as suitable. However, demand, which is conservatively estimated at about 1.6 million ounces annually, has declined substantially over the past decade because of a shift to other alloys and ceramics. The use of gold in dental alloys may increase with affluence in developing countries, or if government or private dental plans pay for its use. At the same time its use will decline in many of the industrialized countries because of the trend toward better dental health as well as payment ceilings by private insurance companies. Nevertheless, the cost of the metal in any dental procedure is only a small fraction of the total cost.

Gold Coins

Bullion coins — issued by governments, and of .995 or .999 fineness, and whose market price is based on their gold content — have long been a favorite of investors because of their purity and marketability. For many years South Africa's Krugerrand had the bulk of the market. But since the mid-1980s, when several governments banned imports of South African coins, market share has shifted, with Canada, the United States, and Mexico, among others, making major gains. Demand for gold coins in a specific market reflects the price of gold, applicable taxes (some governments place a tax on the purchase of coins but not of gold bars), general economic conditions, and confidence in paper currency. Some countries have issued commemorative coins in the hope of appealing to collectors. In recent years demand has been highest for .9999 fineness coins such as the Canadian Maple Leaf.

Investment

Investment demand for gold reflects opportunities and attitudes. For much of the 1970s gold attracted investors in North America and Europe because interest rates provided a poor return relative to inflation. During much of the 1980s interest rates were high compared to inflation, and gold was not a premier investment, especially since supplies were increasing. As well, the stock market offered substantial opportunities for high returns.

Nevertheless, worldwide demand for gold as an investment has grown over the past decade, particularly in the Far East, Latin America, and the Middle East. Growth in these areas has more than offset sales by North American and European investors who have been switching to alternative financial assets.

A number of factors suggest that gold's attractiveness as an investment will almost certainly improve during the remainder of the decade. Concerns about the international monetary structure will almost certainly increase investor demand for gold. Moreover, real interest rates will likely be lower than in the 1980s because of the slowdown in the North American economy. Lower interest rates will increase the attractiveness of gold as a financial asset.

It is important to note that gold has never really caught on as an investment in the United States, the world's largest market. Owning gold bullion was prohibited between 1934 and 1975, so Americans do not have the history of gold ownership that Europeans have. Moreover, the experience of holding gold as a long-term investment in the 1980s has not been rewarding. However, the investment market for gold in the United States has been growing. There are about $3 billion assets in U.S. gold mutual funds. Moreover, demand for gold coins has been increasing in the United States, although the vast majority of purchasers are small investors.

And then there are the countries that were part of the Soviet Union. Their citizens face housing shortages in all major centers. Their antiquated agricultural and transportation infrastructure has left crops rotting in the fields or spoiling en route to markets. Their factories, like Eastern Europe's, are for the most part obsolete and uncompetitive by Western standards, producing shoddy goods. Their currency has no value beyond their borders. While moves have been made to allow a market economy to develop, the widespread underground economy continues to fill the gaps the official sector is unable to fill.

How these countries will solve their long-term problems is anyone's guess. But what is certain is that they cannot solve their problems on their own. They need Western technology and expertise to modernize their economies. Such a program would likely take several decades. Foreign investment is needed, but few investors are willing to make an investment that generates publicity but not dividends. Most investors will want a return on their investment, one that can be converted into other currencies and that they can repatriate or reinvest outside the former Soviet Union. To attract investment on a large scale, these countries will have to provide a means that will allow investors to take a portion of their profits out of the country as dividends in a currency that has some value. Proposals have been made by Western governments to establish a ruble stabilization fund. The ruble would be pegged against a basket of Western currencies and the stabilization fund would be used to buy and sell rubles to keep their value stable against other currencies. Nevertheless, the devaluations of the ruble that accompanied political reform are still fresh in the mind of the citizens of the former Soviet Union. Given the opportunity, many will turn to gold as a means of protecting their savings simply because of tradition and few alternatives.

A Summary of Supply and Demand
Taken alone or together, the components that are part of supply and demand suggest that gold prices will move higher over the next several years.

On the supply side, mine production is near or at its peak and will begin a decline. Similarly, sales from what used to be the Soviet Union will almost certainly be pale compared with the sales of the latter half of the 1980s and the first few years of the 1990s, a reflection of low reserves and inefficient production practices.

Official sales or sales from central banks will

probably remain at recent levels. We do not pretend to be able to forecast what central banks will do, but our best guess is that they will continue to do as they have in the past. Of course, they would likely increase their sales at much higher prices. But even doing that would reflect their then-current policies.

The amount of scrap is difficult to predict but should remain in a range of 8 million to 12 million ounces per year. For our purposes we are estimating 10 million ounces.

The gold derivative markets should remain active. Nevertheless, many gold loans are now in the repayment stage. As well, when a company sells next year's production forward and delivers this year's production to settle previously made forward contracts, the effect on the spot market is nil. We expect that gold derivatives will continue to have the effect of increasing supply to the marketplace. But as the practice matures and mine production begins to decline, the trend will reverse.

So while total mine production will probably peak in 1992, total supply probably peaked in 1991. The main trends that will dominate the early 1990s are declines in production, in sales from Eastern bloc countries, and in net derivatives — in other words, declining supply.

In contrast, demand will likely increase, reflecting the needs of the jewelry industry. Gold jewelry sales, while depressed somewhat by the recession in 1990 and 1991, will increase about 3 percent annually through the 1990s. We assume level demand for other forms of fabrication.

For the purposes of our models we have ignored the potential impact of investment demand, which, of course, could be substantial.

What can be seen from table 2 is that the large surpluses of supply over demand that helped depress gold prices during the 1980s will evaporate in the 1990s. The surpluses in the late 1980s were absorbed by investment buyers who were "price makers" — able to choose their levels and let the market come to them.

The next few years will be different. Only a small surplus should be available for investors in 1992. In 1993 that surplus will turn to a deficit. Our model shows that by 1995 that deficit could be as high as

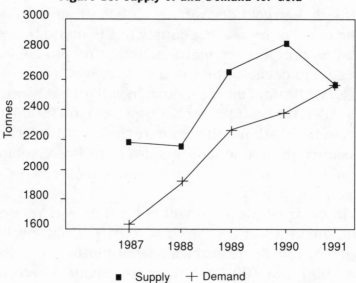

Figure 13: Supply of and Demand for Gold

■ Supply   + Demand

Source: Gold Fields Mineral Services, Goodman & Company

Table 2: Supply and Demand for Gold (millions of ounces)

	1980	1981	1982	1983	1984	1985	1986	1987	1988	1989	1990	1991	1992	1993	1994	1995
Supply																
Mine production	30.92	31.67	33.15	35.89	37.50	39.73	41.66	44.47	49.85	53.14	56.29	57.44	58.13	57.99	57.68	57.26
Communist bloc sales	2.89	9.00	6.53	2.99	6.59	6.75	12.92	9.74	8.46	8.55	13.66	7.27	6.43	5.79	5.79	5.79
Net official sales (purchases)	(7.39)	(8.87)	(2.73)	4.57	2.73	(4.24)	(4.66)	(2.31)	(9.16)	6.98	(2.12)	3.38	3.38	3.38	3.38	3.38
Old gold scrap	15.82	7.84	7.81	9.45	9.36	10.19	15.75	13.89	11.28	11.57	15.75	13.18	13.18	13.18	13.18	13.18
Net gold derivatives	0.0	0.0	0.0	0.0	0.42	2.19	1.99	4.50	8.65	4.60	8.17	1.29	3.22	3.22	3.22	3.22
Total supply	42.24	39.74	44.78	52.85	56.55	54.56	67.61	70.22	68.96	85.62	91.53	82.55	84.33	83.55	83.24	82.82
Demand																
Jewelry	16.51	25.66	30.09	27.07	35.14	38.16	37.55	39.06	49.25	61.31	65.49	67.87	69.23	70.61	72.02	73.46
Other fabrication	13.89	14.11	11.57	13.09	13.28	11.41	19.00	14.37	12.57	13.05	12.96	13.89	13.89	13.89	13.89	13.89
Total fabrication	30.40	39.77	41.67	40.16	48.42	49.58	56.55	53.43	61.82	74.36	78.45	81.76	83.11	84.50	85.91	87.35
Surplus (shortfall) of supply	11.84	(0.03)	3.12	12.70	8.13	4.98	11.06	16.78	7.14	11.25	13.09	0.79	1.21	(0.95)	(2.67)	(4.53)

* Figures have been rounded.
Source: Gold Fields Mineral Services, Goodman & Company

4.5 million ounces. In a deficit scenario, investors would become "price takers," meaning they would have to pay higher prices to induce the sale of gold from a central bank, another investor, or a gold producer.

Figure 13 shows how supply has exceeded demand in recent years. Figure 14 shows supply and demand, excluding sales by the former Soviet Union. Had the former Soviet Union not been a major seller, world demand would have equaled supply in 1990 and exceeded it in 1991 and 1992.

Figure 14: Supply of and Demand for Gold
Excluding Soviet Sales

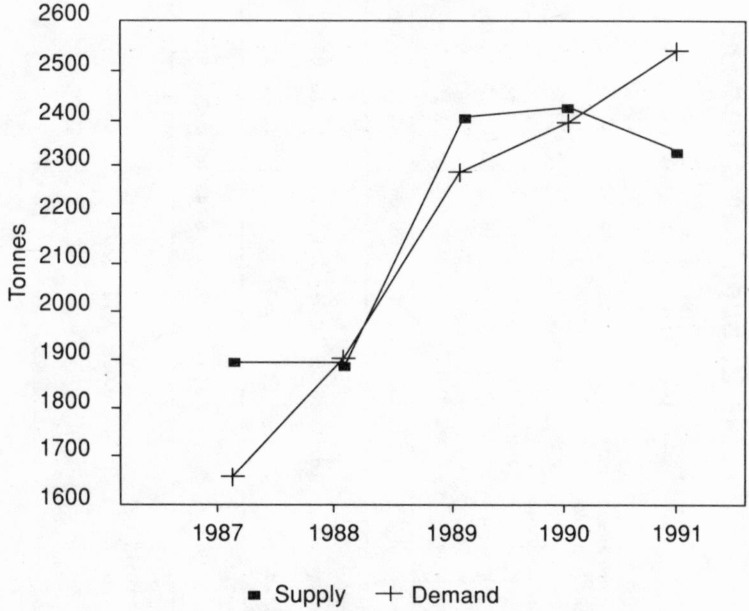

■ Supply   + Demand

Source: Gold Fields Mineral Services, Goodman & Company

Figure 15: Supply of and Demand for Gold
Excluding Soviet Sales and Derivatives

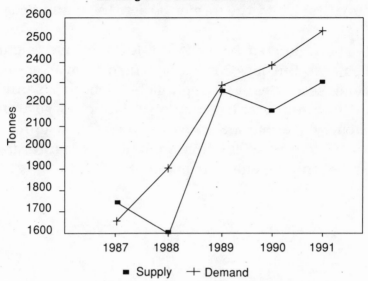

■ Supply + Demand

Source: Gold Fields Mineral Services, Goodman & Company

Figure 16: Supply of and Demand for Gold
Goodman & Company forecast

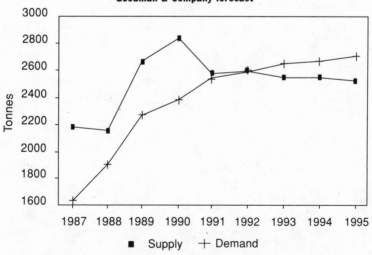

■ Supply + Demand

Source: Gold Fields Mineral Services, Goodman & Company

Figure 15 shows supply and demand, excluding supply sales by the former Soviet Union and hedging.

The unknown factor is the level of investment demand. But lower rates of return from fixed-income securities, very high global debt levels, and an eventual reemergence of inflation as governments try to pursue or maintain economic growth suggest an excellent environment for a marked increase in investment demand.

III. How to Invest in Gold

7. Using Gold Effectively

During the fall of 1990, the world was on red alert. The United States and its allies had sent hundreds of thousands of troops to the Arabian Peninsula girded for war. Oil prices had skyrocketed. The U.S. government, with debts of $3 trillion, faced yet another budget crisis. The U.S. dollar was under pressure in currency markets. The Soviet Union faced bad harvests and economic chaos. Investors faced bear markets in stocks, bonds, and real estate. There were fears of inflation and fears of deflation.

With such turmoil in the background, and given gold's traditional uses as a hedge against inflation, economic and political crises, and currency devaluation, gold should have soared in price. After all, in the past it has often performed well at the very time that stocks and bonds performed poorly. Yet the price of gold languished at about $380 an ounce. Analysts gave several explanations: demand from the jewelry sector was down because of the economic slowdown; sales originating in Middle Eastern nations to finance their mobilizations had kept the price down; and, simply, supply was equal to demand.

What can be concluded is that trying to predict short-term moves in the price of gold is a mug's game. Playing short-term trends can be profitable if one is nimble, but there are no hard and fast rules when it comes to gold and its performance. It has been an excellent crisis hedge in some periods of political turmoil. In others, it has acted poorly.

Similarly, gold has a mixed reputation as a short-term inflation hedge. During the 1970s, when after-tax interest rates lagged behind inflation, gold was king. In much of the 1980s, when real interest rates — the difference between nominal interest rates and inflation rates — were historically high, gold was not a stellar performer. But as the charts of gold prices show, gold's very long-term trend is up, or, conversely, gold holds its value while paper money does not.

In this century governments have attempted to prevent or discourage the use of gold as an investment in various ways, ranging from banning its ownership, as was the case in the United States for four decades, to massive sales of gold in attempts to drive prices lower. Yet no government is above the law of supply and demand. As long as governments create paper money at a faster pace than the supply of goods in the marketplace, prices will rise. And as long as government deficits keep growing, governments will have to print even more money to pay interest on their debt. At some point, confidence in the dollar will be lost by some of the holders of the $3 trillion of U.S. government debt. Even a moderate move from dollars to gold will cause a massive revaluation of the price of gold.

The case in favor of gold as an investment is now probably the best it has been since the mid-1970s, when gold was trading at around $100 an ounce. From an investment point of view, supplies from the mining industry will almost certainly decline over the next few years. While demand from the jewelry industry will, of course, fluctuate with the price of gold and general economic conditions, there seems to be a base price, at around $350, at which the jewelry industry will absorb all gold offered. Should the price drop much below $350, mine production will decrease drastically because fewer mines will be able to operate profitably.

Moreover, gold's status as a reserve currency seems poised to get a boost from the countries that made up the Soviet Union, particularly Russia, which must rebuild its depleted gold reserves. While few governments will encourage their citizens to invest in gold and, in fact, most discourage it, all governments have gold reserves. Some have more than others. Japan, for example, has become the banker to the world because of its massive trade surpluses. However, it has very little gold as a percentage of its foreign-exchange reserves. Should a full-blown economic crisis develop, it is likely Japan would try to salvage some of its reserves by converting U.S. dollars to gold. After all, gold is the ultimate financial asset. It may not pay interest or dividends, but it has no liabilities against it, so it cannot go bankrupt.

Gold is the ultimate money. Ultimate money is ultimate safety. Although gold can be used as an investment on its own merits, its most appropriate use is as part of a diversified investment portfolio. Gold held by itself is a risky investment whose value can fluctuate quite widely. But because gold tends to move independently of other financial assets such as stocks and bonds, it tends to help portfolio performance when combined with other assets. Gold's most important use for investors is as a means of reducing risk.

Although we believe that gold will prove to be a top-performing investment of the 1990s, our experience as investment professionals tells us that portfolios should always be diversified across different classes of assets. Portfolios should emphasize gold, but not to the exclusion of other assets that are good value. To exclude other assets would result in an investor becoming a speculator in gold.

There are two reasons to hold gold in a portfolio. The first is that it will likely provide excellent returns over the remainder of the decade. Returns from gold will likely exceed those from other classes of assets. The second reason is to gain more stable overall returns than you would from holding either gold alone or stocks alone. Returns from gold are not highly correlated with returns from the general stock market. In other words, gold may do well when stocks have low or negative returns, while stocks may perform well when gold's performance is lackluster. Both have positive long-term rates of return. Thus by building a portfolio that includes gold you reduce the month-to-month volatility of your portfolio.

Investment Objectives Are Important

To use gold effectively, you should first determine what it is you are trying to accomplish as well as how much risk you are willing to take. People have different objectives. The most common reasons to hold gold are to to stabilize portfolio returns, as insurance against currency disruptions, as a hedge against inflation, and as a high performer.

Most people should have three investment objectives. The first is to not lose their money. The second is to earn a rate of return that exceeds the long-term rate of inflation by at least three to five percentage points. The third is to do so in a manner that lets them sleep well at night and that does not infringe on the lifestyle they have chosen.

Whereas most people can define their objectives, few can decide how much risk they are willing to take. Unfortunately, too many people discover how much risk they can take only when it is too late — when they are forced to realize losses because they have taken a chance with borrowed funds, or when they learn they have paid too much.

As an investor you have a wide variety of choices when constructing your portfolio. If your objective is income, you can buy government and corporate long-term bonds, treasury bills, or similar instruments. If your objective is growth, you can invest in the stock market, buying shares of senior companies or intermediate and junior companies. You can also invest in preferred shares or real estate or a whole variety of hybrid investments designed to meet specific niche markets or needs. These include zero coupon bonds, convertible preferred shares, and convertible debentures. Finally, you can choose gold.

If you choose gold, you have a wide variety of choices within the category: gold bullion or certificates, gold shares, gold mutual funds, or gold options and gold futures.

An investment in gold can be justified by its long-term performance. When measured over short periods, gold's performance has been mixed, but on average throughout the years the price of gold has easily matched the overall inflation rate. In some areas of the world, against local currencies and in some specific instances, gold has done significantly better than that.

The price of gold is volatile. In the investment business this is called "high variability." Variability is a measure based on calculating the standard deviation of investment returns. The greater the variation in an asset's return, the higher its variability. Treasury bill returns have a low variability. Bond returns are less stable than treasury bill returns but likewise have a lower variability than stocks. Utility stocks are less variable than junior industrial shares. Gold and gold shares have a higher variability than other stocks. (Variability is also sometimes called "risk." It does not, however, mean risk in the conventional sense, as in the risk of losing all your investment.) The best use of gold as an investment medium is as part of a much larger portfolio in which gold accounts for 5 to 20 percent of the total assets. The actual percentage will depend on your preferences and economic conditions. In times of uncertainty, the higher percentage would be appropriate.

While the returns from the gold portion of such a portfolio tend to vary more widely than the rest of the portfolio, the combined returns of the total portfolio are more stable because of gold's countercyclical attribute. Consequently, the total investment portfolio is less volatile than its parts.

Gold is a separate asset class. Its performance is independent of the performance of common stocks of either large or small companies. It moves independently of corporate and government bonds. It has a negative correlation to treasury bills, and an inverse relationship to the U.S. dollar.

As a result, even though gold by itself has a very high standard deviation or volatility (or, as some people believe, risk), it has no correlation or inverse relationship with other classes of investment, and it therefore tends to reduce the variability of the portfolio. This reduction in overall risk affords the investor some peace of mind and increases the return on the overall portfolio, achieving the investment objective we previously set out.

Numerous academic studies have confirmed this

view, covering various markets and using Canadian and South African gold shares as well as bullion. The conclusions generally have been that gold bullion and gold shares have a positive effect on portfolio performance by reducing portfolio volatility. One recent study by Elias Dinenis of the London Business School examined whether the inclusion of gold in the portfolios of 30 United Kingdom pension funds would have improved their performance over the period from 1979 to 1989. "The results suggest that about two-thirds of the pension funds could have improved their performance had they included gold in their portfolios. This is due to the fact that the return on gold is negatively correlated with the portfolio return and, although the inclusion of gold would have slightly reduced the portfolio returns, the reduction in riskiness of the portfolio would have been much greater thus improving the risk-reward relationship of the resulting portfolio."

What to Buy
Gold can be bought in a number of forms: coins, certificates or wafers, shares of gold mining companies, or open-end or closed-end gold funds. These investments can be used as either short- or long-term investments. And though they may fluctuate widely, investors holding them are never in danger of permanent capital loss. Gold cannot go to zero. Neither can a properly chosen diversified portfolio of gold and gold securities.

Yet invariably there are people who say, "I bought

gold and lost money." In fact they usually have not bought gold bullion or a fund or built a diversified portfolio. Rather, they have dabbled in gold options or even futures, derivatives that are essential to the marketplace but a minefield for amateurs. More often they have bought gold mining shares or at least what they thought were gold mining shares. In some cases they bought shares of junior exploration companies, probably the most speculative investments available to the public. Making an investment in gold involves several decisions. The first is to invest. The second is to decide what percentage of assets to invest in gold. The third is to choose the specific investment.

The sleep factor is, of course, an important consideration in deciding what percentage of assets to hold in gold. People who tend to worry a lot about the volatility of their investments may want to keep the portion they hold in gold somewhat low, say 5 percent of their assets. Conversely, individuals who are looking for more than portfolio stability may want to keep a major portion of their assets in gold, even above 20 percent. Most people, however, should take the balanced approach and keep within the range of 5 to 20 percent, leaning toward the higher end of the range when the economic and political scene is unstable.

Gold investments can be classified into four categories: bullion, including bullion coins and certificates; shares of gold producers and companies likely to become gold producers; professionally managed gold portfolios — gold mutual funds and closed-end funds; and derivative products such as gold options and gold futures contracts.

These are summarized here and covered in detail in subsequent chapters. In addition people can buy penny mines or numismatic coins. Both are discussed later.

Gold Bullion
The simplest gold investment is gold itself — bullion, coins, and certificates. These can be purchased through any major bank; the price is widely quoted; and they are instantly liquid. They are available in virtually any amount, ranging from a 5-gram wafer to 400-ounce bars. These are the perfect investment for someone who doesn't want to spend the time or effort analyzing mining shares.

Gold Mining Shares
Gold mining shares, or gold stocks as they are also called, are complex investments, unlike bullion. Gold mining company shares have the highest volatility or risk of virtually any segment of the stock market, even higher than gold itself. Furthermore, gold stocks tend to trade in cycles, and, when gold stocks are in favor with large institutional investors such as mutual funds, banks, and pension funds, shares of the largest gold mining companies achieve collector status because of their scarcity.

Yet many investors prefer shares to bullion because of the potentially higher returns. Prices of gold mining shares tend to outperform bullion during periods of rising prices and fall more than bullion when bullion prices are falling. The relationships between the price of bullion and of mining shares is complex, and each $10 move in the price of an ounce of gold will affect the profits of each mining company differently. No two market cycles behave the same. Generally senior producers — those companies that have significant gold production and usually operate several major mines — have the greatest moves in the early part of a gold cycle simply because they will be the first to benefit from higher prices as they are already in production, and thus have institutional investor acceptance.

Next to move would be those medium-sized production companies that, because of their size and production, do not have institutional investor support but will likely have superior price performance because of their depressed state.

A third group includes junior companies that have made discoveries that are likely to become producing mines but have not yet reached the stage where they generate income. There is a fourth group: speculative junior companies that attract investors who are willing to risk their capital in the hope that their company will strike it rich. While these investors and the capital they provide are important to the mining industry, few understand the risks and the fact that successes are rare.

Most novice investors in senior producing gold mining companies seem to have little understanding of what they have bought. Moreover, most investors tend to move in this market like lemmings and compete with each other to purchase the very few highly visible gold mine securities. They follow the crowd, paying little attention to value. Almost invariably they end up pushing prices beyond reasonable levels and paying too much. Moreover, if prices turn down they are often among the last to sell, holding on in the hope that the price will reverse to the level at which they bought so they can sell and break even. Unfortunately, they base their decisions on emotion rather than fact.

The gold share market outside South Africa is young. The North American gold share market owes its growth to the freeing of the gold price in the early 1970s and fears of revolution in South Africa. Many foreign investors sold their South African gold shares and replaced them with senior North American gold stocks, pushing prices higher. This drive for North American or non–South African production has caused some gold shares to be priced as rare collectibles, rather than as equities whose prices should be tied to value and future earnings and dividends.

The top 10 North American gold mining companies currently annually produce between 9 and 10 million ounces of gold, about 6.5 percent of the world's production. This generates around $3.5 billion of revenue with after-tax earnings of about $450 million. The market capitalization of these 10 companies — the price the stock market places on them — is currently around $15 billion, suggesting an average price-to-earnings ratio of 33, meaning investors are willing to pay $33 for each $1 of earnings. Dividends provide a yield of less than 1 percent.

On average, these 10 companies produce gold for about $245 per ounce as a cash cost, which is about the same as the total North American average. This cash cost excludes the costs of capital and exploration that would be included in a profit calculation. These 10 companies trade at more than 1.5 times their calculated net asset value — the underlying value of the assets behind the company, including its future gold production — using current gold prices.

Conventional financial analysis suggests that investors purchase only stocks whose prices are below the value of the underlying assets, less any liabilities per share. This is called "value investing." It clearly is not evident in the prices of senior gold mining shares.

A significant rise in the gold price is required to justify the current market capitalization of a handful of senior North American gold mining companies. Without such a rise, an investor would overpay for a gold mining share, increasing the variability of the portfolio and reducing the portfolio return. This would, of course, be contrary to the reason for adding gold to a portfolio. The question, then, is: Can you make effective use of gold shares? The answer depends on your knowledge and expertise. The gold share market is for the experts. Notwithstanding the volatility involved, risk is a function of knowledge.

There is a time to purchase individual gold min-

ing companies and a time to sell. The time to purchase may be just before a mining company starts
production from a new mine, provided the price of
the shares has yet to reflect the increased production. Purchasing shares that are at or below the
fundamental value of the company will almost always lead to portfolio gains.

There is much more to analyzing a gold stock
than reading an annual report and press releases
and listening to a stockbroker. Shares must be examined relative to each other. Moreover, each specific property must be analyzed in terms of
production costs, reserves, and the like. This is an
extremely specialized business and requires specialized education honed by experience. An individual investor trying to match the professionals can
accomplish only part of the job. Moreover, the cost
of obtaining and analyzing data is far beyond the
means of most individual investors.

Investment professionals have developed various
techniques for determining the relative values of
mining companies. For example, we at Goodman &
Company developed a valuation model that moni-
tors all classes of gold shares at any projected price
of gold. The model examines the data using the expertise and technical experience of the principals
of the company. It is combined with a visit to each
mining operation. No security is included in a portfolio without this so-called due diligence visit. Even
with this experience and concentrated effort, the
success ratio is never 100 percent.

The purchase of gold mining shares is not for the
uninitiated. However, the rewards, when a pur-

chase is properly executed, can be enormous. The discovery of a gold mine represents the true creation of wealth.

Investment Funds

An investor who wants an exposure to gold and gold shares but who doesn't have the skills, knowledge, or time to analyze gold companies can get professional management using gold mutual funds and closed-end funds. Gold mutual funds are portfolios of gold shares and bullion managed by investment professionals. The managers of such funds decide what mix of bullion and shares will give investors at any given time the best returns with the least amount of risk. They also determine which shares within the share portion of the portfolio have the greatest potential for gain. Closed-end funds are also professionally managed portfolios. Shares of closed-end funds are listed on stock exchanges and are bought and sold in the same way that stocks are.

Few individual investors can match the expertise of the managers of such funds. Many investors, however, prefer to construct their own portfolios. If you do decide to invest directly, do your homework thoroughly and gain a knowledge of all aspects of a company, ranging from the technical aspects of its properties to its ability to raise financing.

Options and Futures

Besides bullion, shares and gold funds, gold investors can deal in gold derivatives — investments based on gold. The largest markets are gold options and futures. They are widely used by mining companies and industrial users to lock in prices and reduce risk. But they are also a speculator's dream, the shortcuts to that pot at the end of the rainbow. Yet they can be a tool used by conservative investors to protect or enhance profits and reduce risk.

A gold option is the right to buy or sell a specific amount of gold — 100 ounces, in the case of the most widely traded Comex option — at a specific price up to a specific date. An option that gives you the right to buy is called a call option. A put option is the right to sell. Options trade on exchanges such as the New York Commodity Exchange, or Comex. The price paid for the option is called the "premium." For example, in mid-November 1990, when gold was trading at $381 an ounce, a call option to buy 100 ounces of gold at $380 an ounce until the third Friday of April 1991 traded at $20.70. If gold jumped to, say, $430 an ounce, before the option expired, the value of the premium would reflect the difference between the exercise price (in this case $380) and the market price (in this case $430) of an ounce of gold, and the investor would make a hefty profit. If, however, gold remained at $378, the option would expire worthless and the investor would lose his or her $20.70 plus commission.

The expectation of hefty profits draws people to the option market. Options are marketable and can be bought and sold before maturity. Options can be used by different types of investors. A speculator hoping for a huge profit might buy options. A conservative investor who wants to benefit from gold but who is unwilling to tie up a large portion of capital buying bullion may choose to invest a small part in options. A holder of gold who believes gold will not move higher over the short term might decide to sell options against his or her gold. The option seller would receive the premium, and thus gain some protection if gold prices move lower. Similarly, someone holding gold might decide to buy a put option to reduce risk. If the price of gold declines, the profit made on the put option would offset the decline in the value of the gold owned.

Gold futures are the obligation to deliver or receive 100 ounces of gold on a specific date. A speculator expecting the price of gold to rise substantially would go "long" in the futures market — in other words, buy gold for future delivery. Conversely, a speculator expecting the price to drop would go "short," or sell gold for future delivery. (In either case, he or she would not actually receive or deliver gold but would sell or buy offsetting contracts prior to the delivery date to cancel out the contracts.) The incentive for a speculator is that only a fraction of the value of the contract has to be put up with the broker as margin, or good faith, money. As a result, an investor could go long 10 gold contracts with a value of $400,000 by putting up only $40,000. (The minimum margin required under commodity exchange rules is less, but most dealers require more than the absolute minimum.) If the price of gold jumps, say, $50 an ounce before the delivery date, the speculator will realize a huge profit. However, if the price of gold declines $10 an ounce, this investor will be down $10,000 and the broker will require that an additional margin equal to that decline be put up immediately. If the margin is not posted, the position will be sold out and the investor will suffer the loss. Gold mining companies often use the futures markets to lock in a price for a portion of their future production.

Most novice investors who dabble in options and futures lose their capital. Derivatives have their uses for professional and sophisticated individual investors, but they are not for beginners and should be considered only by investors who have an understanding of the markets gained through experience.

Penny Mines
Unfortunately, the first experience many people have with investing in the stock market involves penny mines — highly speculative securities often sold to unsophisticated, unsuspecting investors by telephone. Their name comes from the fact that they are priced in pennies, the idea being that if a penny stock goes up in value by a few pennies, it is a significant percentage increase. Penny mines are almost always sold on the basis of their exploration prospects, so generally there are no income-generating assets behind the company. Buyers of these stocks are, in effect, gamblers. However, many of the people who buy them don't realize that they are gambling. Penny mines should not be confused with real mining investments.

The money raised through issues of most penny

mines, after expenses and commissions, is used for exploration. In reality, very much of the money raised is actually used for commissions paid to brokers, issue expenses, property costs and legal and audit costs. The end result is that very little of the funds raised is put into the ground.

Exploration is, of course, a high-risk business. Few penny mining companies find ore bodies that are developed into mines, and in most cases investors lose all or most of their capital.

Some penny mines trade over the counter, meaning they are not listed on a stock exchange. Often the dealer who is the underwriter of the penny mine issue will control the market in the shares, selling at one price and buying at a much lower price. In many cases there is no real secondary market, or after market, for these shares. In other words, no dealer other than the underwriter has any interest in the shares and is willing to trade them. An investor who buys them is often stuck with them.

Other penny mines trade on a stock exchange such as the Vancouver Stock Exchange and consequently are likely to be more liquid than penny mines that trade over the counter. Even so, they are still risky and not suitable for people whose key investment objective is preservation of capital and restful sleep.

Numismatic Coins
Two types of gold coins are available to investors. The first is the bullion coin, which trades at a small premium over the price of its bullion content. The

second is the numismatic coin, which is prized for its scarcity rather than for its gold content. Numismatic coins can trade at prices many times the value of their gold content. As such they are a very expensive way of owning gold and aren't really a gold investment in the same way that gold bars, gold coins, and certificates are.

Moreover, numismatic coins are relatively illiquid, meaning that they cannot be easily sold. Whereas a holder of a Canadian Maple Leaf can sell that coin through a bank branch anytime and receive a price effectively equal to the value of the gold in the coin, holders of numismatic coins must deal with a coin dealer or an auction house, where the price received will depend on the condition of the coin, its scarcity, and the price other collectors are willing to pay.

A dealer will consider the coin as merchandise to be bought at a wholesale price and sold at retail. Often the price at which a dealer will buy a numismatic coin is only 70 or 80 percent of the price at which the coin will be resold. The discount will vary with the demand for a specific coin and the volatility of the market. In comparison, the spread between the buying and selling prices of a one-ounce Maple Leaf is only about 1.5 percent.

Conclusion

Gold can be used in a portfolio to stabilize returns, as insurance, as a hedge against inflation, and as a speculation. Your choice of bullion and coins, gold shares, gold mutual funds and closed-end funds, and gold options and futures depends on how much effort you want to put into analyzing and monitoring individual investments, and how much risk you are willing to accept against the promise of high returns. Bullion has the least risk; its price can vary widely, but it will never go to zero value. At the opposite end of the spectrum are options and futures. These offer the highest potential returns and the highest probability of wiping out all your capital. Gold mining shares can provide higher returns than bullion. The wise investor, however, will spread his or her risk among several mines. Gold mutual funds and gold closed-end funds are a good compromise for most people because they provide professional management, diversification, and liquidity.

8. Owning Bullion

The easiest way to own gold is to buy bullion. It is available in bars and wafers, bullion coins, and in certificate form, all of which trade at prices based on the widely quoted 400-ounce bar of .995 or higher fineness.

Bullion bars and wafers, bullion coins, and certificates each have their own advantages and disadvantages. However, all represent an investment in gold itself. All are instantly convertible into cash and internationally negotiable. Your choice among the three basic types reflects your objectives and purpose for buying gold. Individuals using gold as a portfolio asset would likely choose bars and wafers or certificates, using a dealer as custodian. Those who want to have physical possession of their gold for purposes of liquidity or privacy and who do not want their gold held by or in a bank for safekeeping might opt for bullion coins or wafers or small bars.

Bullion, coins, and certificates are considered capital assets for tax purposes. Consequently, gains and losses are subject to capital gains treatment. However, almost every province or state applies provincial or state sales taxes to purchases of gold coins but not to purchases of bars or wafers. Many gold buyers therefore prefer bullion bars and wafers over coins.

Nevertheless, coins are the choice of individuals who want gold in a form whose weight and quality are recognizable worldwide and are, consequently, completely liquid. It is quite common for people who live in jurisdictions that place sales taxes on coins to buy them in jurisdictions such as Alberta or Nevada, which have no tax on coins, and store them there, thus avoiding these taxes. In fact, it is quite common for investors who live in jurisdictions where ownership of gold is prohibited or taxed to buy and store their gold in markets such as London.

In Canada, gold bullion and gold coins that are at least 99.5 percent pure are considered financial instruments by the federal government for Goods and Services Tax purposes, and as such are exempt from GST, just as an investment in a stock or bond is exempt from GST. Bullion, coins, and certificates are also treated differently from other capital assets if purchased with borrowed funds. Generally, interest paid on funds borrowed for investment purposes, such as to buy stocks or bonds, is deductible for tax purposes because the investment is made for the purpose of earning income. But gold, gold coins, or a gold certificate cannot pay dividends or interest. Consequently, interest on money borrowed to buy gold cannot be deducted for tax purposes in Canada. If you are planning to buy gold with borrowed funds, you might be able to restructure your finances so that you buy gold with your own capital. Then you can borrow against the gold to buy other investments that meet the criteria for interest deductibility.

Bullion Bars and Wafers

Bullion bars are available in a wide variety of sizes ranging from a one-gram wafer (there are 31.15 grams in a troy ounce), sold more as a jewelry item than as an investment, to the 400-ounce London Good Delivery Bar. From an investment point of view, the range is 5 grams to 400 ounces. Each bar is stamped with the name of the refiner. Investors have their choice of buying in either metric or imperial weights. Metric sizes are 5-, 10-, 20-, and 500-gram wafers and a 1000-gram or 1-kilo bar, all of which are .9999 fineness. Ounce measures are half-, 1-, 2-, 5-, and 10-ounce wafers, all of which are .9999 fineness. In addition gold is available in 100-ounce and 400-ounce bars of either .9999 or .995+ fineness.

The price of gold is quoted by dealers on a bid and an ask or offer basis. The bid price is the price at which the dealer will buy gold. The ask or offer price is the price at which the dealer will sell a 400-

ounce bar of .995+ fineness. If a purchase is for smaller amounts, the buyer will pay a premium based on the size of wafer or bar purchased. The premium reflects the costs of manufacturing smaller bars and wafers. The premium is payable when the individual purchases gold but not on the resale back to the dealer (see table 3).

The premium as a percentage of the price of gold can be substantial for small amounts. For example, on the purchase of a 5-gram wafer, which has fine ounce content of, or contains, 0.161 ounces of gold, the premium per ounce is $50, or $8.05 per wafer, using a recent price list of Bank of Nova Scotia. If a 10-gram wafer is purchased, the premium is $25 an ounce, or $8.05 per wafer. For a kilo bar — 32.148 ounces of gold — the premium is $3.10 an ounce, or $99.66 per bar. On a half-ounce wafer, the premium is $20 an ounce, or $10 per wafer. For a 400-ounce bar of .9999 fineness a premium of $1 an ounce would be paid. No premium is payable on a 400-ounce bar of .995+ fineness.

If an investor takes delivery, he or she may pay a delivery charge covering shipping costs and a small commission on transactions. In early 1992, the Bank of Nova Scotia, one of the largest dealers in North America, charged 0.25 percent on amounts up to $5,000, with a minimum charge of $5, and 0.125 percent on amounts of $5,000 or more, with a minimum charge of $10.

Most buyers of small amounts choose to keep their gold with the dealer rather than take delivery. That way they avoid delivery charges as well as the cost

Table 3: Weights of Gold Bars and Wafers Generally Available Through Major Gold Dealers and Premiums Charged on Purchase

Weight	Bar Charge or Premium per Ounce ($US)
400 ounce bar	nil
100 ounce bar	$1.50-$2.00
10 ounce bar	$4.00-$8.00
5 ounce wafer	$4.75-$9.00
2 ounce wafer	$9.00-$10.00
1 ounce wafer	$6.00-$10.00
½ ounce wafer	$20.00
Kilo bar	$2.00-$3.10
500 gram bar	$3.00
250 gram bar	$4.00
100 gram wafer	$5.00-$11.00
50 gram wafer	$6.00-$12.50
20 gram wafer	$9.50-$15.50
10 gram wafer	$15.00-$25.00
5 gram wafer	$35.00-$50.00

Bar charges or premiums per ounce are charged when an investor makes a purchase. These charges vary widely among dealers. In addition, dealers will charge a commission on transactions which, depending on the dealer, may be a percentage (0.25% on amounts less than $5,000, 0.125% on larger amounts) or a charge per ounce. Minimum commissions vary as well.

Sources: Bank of Nova Scotia, Canadian Imperial Bank of Commerce, and Toronto Dominion Bank

of an assay, which would be required when reselling gold back to a dealer. They also avoid the cost of having to insure their gold if they held it privately.

However, buyers should be aware that there are two types of storage accounts, depending on the dealer. An allocated account is a segregated account, which means that your holding is segregated from gold belonging to other investors and to the dealer. With an unallocated account, your gold is pooled with that of other investors and is a liability of the dealer. The difference between the two types of accounts may seem minor but it can be very important if the dealer runs into financial difficulties.

Dealer costs for storage and safekeeping are nominal. Bank charges for allocated storage and safekeeping in early 1992 were 0.375 percent on the first $50,000 and 0.125 percent on the balance, payable on the anniversary of the opening of the storage account, with a minimum charge of $25 per annum.

People who have a large amount of gold, say, several hundred thousand dollars' worth, will be able to save on storage and safekeeping costs by moving their gold to a safety deposit box. They are then responsible for insuring their gold against loss. The cost, however, will be small.

Certificates
The alternative to buying the actual metal is buying a gold certificate. The advantage of certificates is their lower storage and administration costs, and

lower premiums than those charged for bullion for small amounts. It is important to note that certificates for gold are not necessarily backed by an equivalent amount of bullion. Consequently, investors who buy certificates must realize that the dealer will not have a gold bar or wafer with the investor's name on it in a vault backing that certificate.

Investors should buy dealer-backed certificates only from dealers who are strong financially.

Certificates can be converted into bullion at any time, with delivery within 30 business days. Depending on the issuer, certificates may be negotiable worldwide.

Certificates can be purchased for any weight of gold of one ounce or more. Since fractional weights to three decimal places are available, purchases can be in dollar amounts of, say, $500 or $1,000, as opposed to purchases by weight. This also gives investors the option of purchasing gold monthly or quarterly using specific dollar amounts. Commission charges are the same as with bullion — 0.25 percent on amounts less than $5,000 and 0.125 percent on amounts $5,000 or more.

There are also storage and administration charges. The Bank of Nova Scotia's are three cents per 100 ounces per day for the first 2,000 ounces or just under $11 a year for 100 ounces; two cents per 100 ounces per day on the next 8,000 ounces; and one cent per 100 ounces per day on the balance, with a minimum charge of $5 a year. Storage charges are payable when a certificate is sold or exchanged for bullion, when a portion of a certificate is sold, or when a certificate is reregistered in another name or split into smaller denominations. When a certificate is exchanged for bullion, the holder can expect to pay a manufacturing charge on the bars requested as well as shipping costs if applicable.

Bullion Coins

Because of sales taxes, gold bullion coins are a lot less popular in North America than in other parts of the world. Nevertheless, they are popular with some investors because they are small investments, because they can be stored easily, and because of their small, readily marketable weights. They suit investors who want to keep their gold. Investors who intend to make a substantial investment in gold coins could take delivery in one of the provinces or states (such as Alberta or Florida) that exempt coins from sales tax, and store the coins there. Of course, if a resident of one of these jurisdictions orders coins for delivery elsewhere, he is responsible for sales taxes.

The most popular gold coin in Canada, and in many other countries as well, is the Canadian $50 Maple Leaf, which is .9999 fineness and which has fine ounce content of one ounce of gold. The Maple Leaf is legal tender, and its gold content is guaranteed by the Government of Canada. It is available in three other sizes: the $20 Maple Leaf contains one-half ounce of gold; the $10 Maple Leaf contains one-quarter ounce of gold; and the $5 Maple Leaf contains one-tenth of an ounce of gold. The dollar values stamped on the coins are nominal, and no one would spend them at their face value. Rather, the prices at which an investor buys and sells are based on the price of bullion. For example, when gold was bid $350 and offered at $353.50, the one-ounce Maple Leaf was quoted at bid $357, offered at $364. What this means is that a buyer of the $50 Maple Leaf would pay $364 for a single coin, the premium covering the manufacturing cost and the dealer's markup. Part of this premium would be recovered when the investor sells the coin. The premiums on smaller coins are higher (see table 4).

In the United States the coin to own is the American Eagle. It, too, is legal tender, and its gold content is guaranteed by the U.S. government. It is available in one-ounce, half-ounce, quarter-ounce, and one-tenth-ounce sizes. Its premiums are somewhat different from the Maple Leaf's. When the Maple Leaf was bid at $357 and offered at $364 in Toronto, Republic National Bank of New York was quoting the one-ounce American Eagle at bid $360.35, offered at $362.50.

Canada and the United States are two of more than a dozen countries that produce gold bullion coins. Other popular gold coins include the British Sovereign, Austrian 100 Coronas, Mexican 50 Pesos, and the Australian Nugget. Premiums vary from coin to coin. The first country to issue gold bullion coins was South Africa with its Krugerrand, and for many years it dominated the market. However, it fell out of favor in recent years because of sanc-

Table 4: Gold Bullion Coins

The most popular gold coins in North America include the Canadian Maple Leaf, the American Eagle, the U.K. Britannia, the Chinese Panda, 100 Austrian Corona, and 50 Mexican Peso. Availability, however, will vary widely among dealers. This table shows the premiums quoted on several coins by one Canadian dealer.

Coin	Size	Premium over spot bid price	Premium over spot offering price
Gold Maple Leaf	1 ounce	2.5%	4.0%
Gold Maple Leaf	½ ounce	4.0%	6.5%
Gold Maple Leaf	¼ ounce	6.0%	9.5%
Gold Maple Leaf	¹⁄₁₀ ounce	8.0%	17%
Gold Chinese Panda	1 ounce	4.0%	8.0%
Gold Chinese Panda	½ ounce	6.0%	11.0%
Gold Chinese Panda	¼ ounce	8.0%	15.0%
Gold Chinese Panda	¹⁄₁₀ ounce	12.0%	20.0%
Gold Chinese Panda	¹⁄₂₀ ounce	20.0%	45.0%
Gold Russian Chervonetz	0.25 ounce	–1.0%	3.0%

tions against South Africa, and few dealers in North America carry it today. Nevertheless, investors who bought the Krugerrand have no difficulty selling it for the value of its gold content less a small discount to cover the cost of melting. Gold is gold, and once melted and recast there is no way of telling whether it was originally mined in Canada, South Africa, or anywhere else.

There are some charges associated with purchasing gold coins. You can expect to pay the same commissions you would pay when buying bullion — 0.25 percent on amounts less than $5,000, using the Scotiabank's schedule, for example, and 0.125 percent for amounts of $5,000 or more.

If you choose to leave your coins with the bank in allocated storage and safekeeping, the charges would also be the same as for bullion — 0.375 percent on the first $50,000 and 0.125 percent on any amount in excess of $50,000. The minimum charge is $25 a year. The charges are based on the market value of your account on the anniversary of its opening.

You can also buy coin certificates, which can be converted into coin for delivery within five business days on payment of storage and administration charges. The storage charges are two-tenths of a cent per ounce per day or a minimum of $5 per year.

Choosing a Dealer
There are a limited number of dealers through whom you can buy or sell gold. In Canada the largest dealer is the Bank of Nova Scotia. The Canadian Imperial Bank of Commerce and Toronto Dominion Bank are also very active in the precious-metals markets. The market is complex, and most investors are best off doing business with dealers either directly or through their own banking institutions.

If someone offers you gold at a special price, walk away. There have been several scams in the United States involving gold sales by mail or by telephone. The price of gold is quoted internationally, and everyone is on an equal footing. If you are going to buy or sell bullion, deal only with the large, long-established, reputable dealers. Commissions charged, while negligible, vary among institutions, as do storage and safekeeping charges.

9. Investing in Shares

The price of bullion will undoubtedly rise over the next few years, yet higher gains will likely be made in shares of some gold producers. Even if gold prices remain steady, share prices of gold mining companies that can increase their underlying values — through acquisitions, discoveries, and increased production — will rise, giving higher returns than bullion. That's the key reason for an investor to look at shares of gold producers as an alternative to bullion. The objective of the investor in gold shares is, or should be, to seek out those companies likely to give better performance than bullion.

A key factor to consider is that movements in gold shares only partially reflect the price of gold bullion. Gold shares, of course, will move up and down as a group in sympathy with the price of bullion. But gold share prices are often more volatile than the price of gold because of the leverage, or effect, a move in the price of gold has on the value of a company's production and its cash flow. Take the case of a rise in the price of gold from $400 to $425 an ounce. The increase is 6.25 percent. But for a company whose cash costs of production are $250 an ounce, a $25 increase in the price to $425 raises that company's cash profit margin from $150 to $175 an ounce or by 15.25 percent.

Other factors include the company's ability to find, expand, and develop ore reserves or acquire other companies at a discount to their underlying assets. Similarly, politics can affect the value of gold shares. For instance, senior North American gold company shares outperformed South African gold stocks as a group when many North American and European institutional investors decided to divest their holdings of South African shares because of the political situation there and replaced their holdings with North American shares.

As well, no two gold mining companies are alike. Indeed, the range of investment quality among gold shares is extremely wide, from senior producers to junior exploration companies whose only association with gold is in their promotional material. There are literally hundreds of mining companies with gold properties. Many are junior exploration companies with properties that may or may not produce gold. Investors contemplating these should realize that there is a difference between speculating on whether a company will find gold and investing in a gold mining company that is producing gold or has a property soon to go into production. The ex-

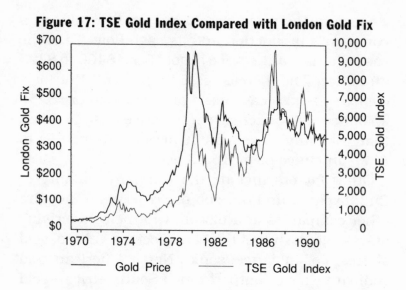

Figure 17: TSE Gold Index Compared with London Gold Fix

perience of the industry is that the probability of any one junior exploration company finding an economic gold deposit is very small.

Money can be made in these juniors, particularly during "hot" gold markets when a speculative frenzy can develop in junior exploration companies. But money can also be lost. An investment in a junior exploration company should not be equated with an investment in gold bullion or in shares of a producing gold company.

The investor who is interested in shares of producers as an alternative to bullion and who has the time and skills to analyze securities has several dozen companies from which to choose. Sources of information include annual and quarterly reports as well as brokerage house analytical reports. Other sources of information include newspapers such as the *Northern Miner* and the daily business press. Professional investors, brokers, and those individuals who can afford the cost and want up-to-the-minute information flows can get access to wire services to provide them with the latest information.

Analyzing gold shares involves a different set of criteria than analyzing other stocks. The objective in analyzing any stock group is to seek out companies that are undervalued. But measures of value for gold shares differ from the measures applied to stocks in general.

The biggest mystery of the gold share market to novice investors and many successful investors in other segments of the market is the apparent overvaluation of North American gold equities relative to other securities. Many North American investors have always stayed clear of gold stocks because they generally look expensive by traditional investment standards, which measure the price of a share relative to earnings, cash generated, and value of shareholder's equity or ownership in a company. Gold shares trade at high price to earnings, cash flow, and book value multiples.

In fact, shares of many gold producers are overvalued based on detailed analyses. But there are many excellent values as well. It is up to the individual investor to determine which is which. To do this, the investor can rely on his or her own detailed studies, or on information supplied by brokers.

Price to Earnings and Price to Cash Flow Multiples

Traditional analytical measures used in securities analysis don't generally work when it comes to analyzing gold stocks. Measures of value used in resource analysis include price to earnings and price to cash flow multiples — the price an investor pays for each dollar of earnings or each dollar of cash flow. (Cash flow is a measure of cash available to a company from its operations. It is calculated by adding back to earnings expenses or charges that don't involve actual cash payments, such as depreciation of equipment and depletion of ore bodies.)

There are four reasons that price to earnings and cash flow multiples do not give a fair valuation of a gold producer's value.

1. Many gold mining companies have properties or other assets that are not at the time producing gold. As a result, these assets do not produce earnings or cash flow. Share prices of such companies should include a premium for these assets, which will be producing gold at some point in the future and generating cash flow. Applying a standard industry-wide multiple to these companies is not prudent because it will ignore and undervalue these valuable assets.

2. Many gold companies have large cash balances on their balance sheets. This money is invested in, say, treasury bills to earn interest. Applying a high multiple to interest earnings would,

of course, overvalue this income. For example, if a company had $100 million in cash invested at an interest rate of 10 percent and paid a 40 percent income tax rate, its after-tax earnings on the cash balance would be $6 million. Applying a multiple of 20 times earnings (conservative by any gold market standards) to the $6 million earnings would value the $100 million of cash at $120 million when it should be valued only at its face value.

3. Because of the volatility of gold prices, many gold companies use the futures market to hedge the prices they get on their production. By using futures they lock in a price on the gold they produce that may prove better (or worse) than the market price in subsequent months or even years. While forward selling is prudent management for high-cost operations, it does not deserve a high multiple. Most companies sell a fraction of their production forward for one to three years at a time. In periods of declining gold prices, companies that sell forward will do better than companies that do not hedge and that sell their production at the market. Conversely, companies that hedge by selling forward will not do as well as companies that sell production at the market when prices are rising. If a company has done well with its hedging program, it will benefit for a finite period of the length of the contract (usually one to three years). If a company earns more than other gold companies because of a forward sale, and a premium multiple is applied to those earnings, then the stock market will be expecting

that company to outperform the gold market for the entire life of its assets. This would be true if the company had only three years of reserves, after which the mine would cease to operate. However, most companies have more than that level.

Undoubtedly, any company that can continuously and successfully forecast the gold price over a long term will deserve a premium multiple. At the same time, anybody (or any company) that can continuously and successfully forecast the gold price over a long term doesn't need a mine, only a good broker. The conclusion is that paying a high multiple cannot be justified for a relatively short-term hedging program.

4.   An even more dramatic effect of earnings distortion results from gold loans, another widely used form of hedging by gold producers. A gold loan, as the name suggests, is a loan of gold to a gold producer from a bank. The bank, instead of lending the mining company cash, lends the company gold, which the bank sells on the company's behalf to provide the mining company with cash. The company repays the bank in gold out of subsequent years' production.

Gold loans work because the price of gold in the futures market is always more than the price in the spot or current market. The reason is that gold, while rare, is far from scarce as a financial asset and can always be borrowed. Consequently, the spread between a spot and futures price is, in effect, the cost of money over the time period. In other words, the price of the future contract, say, for delivery in three months is not less than the price of gold today, plus the interest that would be earned over the next three months if that gold were sold and invested in treasury bills until settlement of the futures contract. The difference between the price of a futures contract and the spot price of gold has always been positive and is called the "contango."

A bank, at the same time it lends the company gold, would sell an equivalent amount in the forward market, thus earning the contango. Because the bank has this spread locked in, it can charge a much lower rate on the gold loan than it would for cash.

Take, for example, the company that borrows gold at $360 an ounce on a one-year basis. Its banker would sell an equivalent amount of gold in the futures market one year forward at $375, giving it a 4 percent premium or, in other words, locking in a 4 percent return for the one year. Because it has this profit locked in, it would have to charge the borrower only 4 percent to make a return of 8 percent on the loan. Of course the borrower would be responsible for delivering one ounce of gold to the bank in one year. If the gold price was to rise to above the $375 price, the borrower would have been better to borrow in cash.

Gold loans affect earnings and cash flow two ways. First, they give a false impression of the cost of capital. Consider two companies that each have 50 percent of the same asset. One has a $100-million gold loan and the other has $100 million of conventional bank debt. All other things being identical, both companies should be worth the same. If one considers earnings and cash flow, the company with the gold loan looks better, since it would have to pay $4 million in interest costs. In contrast, the company with the conventional debt would pay $8 million in interest costs. What is not reflected in income statements is the fact that the company that paid $4 million gave up to the bank the $4-million contango it could have earned itself. This charge is not reflected in income statements.

Second, accountants like to treat gold loans as deferred revenue. So while the company has the use of revenues from future production in the year the loan is made, the sale is recorded only when the gold loan is repaid. This accounting procedure can distort earnings. For example, if a company borrowed gold several years ago when the price was $450 an ounce and repaid the loan when gold traded at $360, its income statement would state that the company sold gold this year at $450 per ounce rather than $360. As this repayment is a non-cash transaction (the gold is repaid in ounces), it tends to overstate (or understate) earnings. Gold loan transactions can be even more complex to interpret when a company borrows gold at 4 percent and then reinvests the cash at 8 percent. The investor or analyst must understand the transaction fully to avoid applying a gold multiple to earnings that do not deserve a gold multiple.

Analyzing Gold Shares

Analyzing gold shares is complicated, and there are no shortcuts. Data released by companies must be examined closely. One of the major lessons learned by analysts over the past three decades is that reserves, as reported by companies, cannot always be accepted at their face value. Some companies may report 5 years of reserves when in fact they have 40 years or more. Others may report 10 years of reserves when in fact they have only 5 years.

Investing in gold mining shares is risky at the best of times. But investors can cut their risks by making sure that the data they have are accurate and complete. When a mining company buys another mining company, the deal is usually contingent on a period of due diligence to allow the acquiring company an opportunity to inspect the operations and examine the reserves of the company being acquired. This inspection allows the buyer to determine if, in fact, everything is as represented. A due diligence examination is a normal part of acquisitions in the mining business but is not part of the analysis done by many investors and some brokers and analysts.

Nevertheless, as part of the analysis a professional investor should make a property visit. Otherwise he or she could be working with data that will result in incorrect conclusions. The most sophisticated valuation model is only as good as the numbers that are fed into it. Indeed, before buying any gold stock, a due diligence property visit is required. The information that can be gleaned makes the property visit the single most important element in the valuation of gold stocks. In some cases a property visit can provide warnings to head for the hills. In other cases it can show potential that could not be determined from an analysis of printed corporate material.

The Property Visit
Some mining companies believe that a visit by a professional investor involves just a trip out to the mine, a look at the operation, lunch, a couple of drinks, and a trip home. This type of property visit is truly a waste of time. A proper visit should also include a review of the property's operations, its reserves, and its actual versus projected costs, and an examination of the five-year plan for that mine. Being on site gives the analyst advantages that aren't available if he or she simply sits in an office reading the data.

Although it is not within the scope of the analyst's visit to recalculate reserves, he or she will review reserves by looking at the cross-sections of the deposit, reviewing the underlying geological assumptions that the company has used in arriving at its reserve figures, and, of course, asking a lot of questions of the people responsible for the operation. It goes without saying that the analyst looking at the operations must have the training and experience to understand them. Mining companies are generally willing to have analysts examine their properties. However, it is a waste of time if the analyst hasn't the knowledge to interpret what is seen. If the property has a production history, the analyst should compare actual production numbers against previous forecasts. Discrepancies between the two can indicate to the analyst the potential error in his or her own forecasts. The analyst will draw on his or her experience and knowledge of the industry when examining the costs of the operation. The analyst would also compare the cost per ton against budgets and against the costs experienced by similar mines.

A property visit also gives the analyst the opportunity to assess management — an important part of the evaluation that can't be done by reading an annual report — and to determine if the operation is well managed. Bad management can ruin a good property.

Based on the visit, the analyst will produce an assessment of the operation, a production forecast, and an estimate of the life of the mine. This estimate should be on the conservative side, given the nature of gold mining and the likelihood of surprises as the ore body is exploited. In the mining business it is far better to err on the side of safety.

The Financial Analysis

Once the property visit is complete, the analyst can construct a financial analysis or valuation. The first step in the analysis is to make production and cost projections for the estimated life of the company's assets. Experience and knowledge are key to the analyst's ability to make estimates involving intangibles such as ultimate mine life and changes in ore grades and costs as the mine deepens.

The starting point for the analysis is the current market price for gold. Adjustments that reflect expected changes in the gold price are made at a later stage in the analysis. Similarly, the mining company's current costs would be used in the analysis with adjustments made to reflect predictable infrastructural cost increases such as those in stripping or haulage costs.

To offset the fact that no factor for inflation is used in the gold price or the cost estimates, a discount rate that has been adjusted for inflation is used in the analysis. Because 10-year projections are made for most operations, we would use the U.S. long-term bond interest rate of 8 percent minus a 5 percent long-term inflation rate to give us an inflation-adjusted discount rate of 3 percent. To this we would add a 2 percent risk premium, which in turn gives a 5 percent discount rate for the valuation.

Once all of the assumptions are made, the cash flow can be forecast for each year over the estimated life of the property. Combining the analyses of all the company's properties allows the analyst to value the whole company.

We calculate cash flow in our valuation model as follows:

First, we determine net revenues for each year by multiplying the expected production in ounces by the gold price. From this we subtract the following:

- Cash costs of production. (These estimates stem from the property visit.)
- Cash overhead costs. (These estimates are based on historical costs and discussions with management.)
- Taxes payable. (These are estimated from discussions with the mining company's financial managers and from the analyst's experience.)
- Ongoing capital expenditures and mine site exploration. (These are estimates based on discussions with mine management. The exploration expenditures used in the analysis are only those applicable to the reserves forecast. If a company has five years of reserves and we feel that the mine will exist for seven years, we would include as an exploration expense only those dollars needed to find the final two years.)

It is important to note that the key in each of these components is cash.

These future cash flows are then discounted to present value by the real 5 percent discount rate, as previously described. We do not deduct interest payments from the cash flow, as this would be double-accounting the debt. The sum of these discounted cash flows is then added to produce a net present value of the company's gold assets. The net present value of the company is the sum of the values of the gold assets plus the values of the company's other assets, such as corporate cash and non-gold assets, less the company's debt. To estimate the net present value per share of the company, we divide the net present values of the company by the fully diluted number of shares outstanding (the actual number of shares outstanding plus shares that may be issued because of options or other commitments).

This analysis gives the net present value of the company at the current price of gold. The next step is to determine the value of the company using a range of gold prices. These figures will show how sensitive the net present value is to changes in the gold price.

The investor's objective is to buy shares trading at a discount to net present value. However, sometimes a stock trading at a premium to its net present value makes more sense than one trading at a discount because the leverage of the net present value to the gold price is very high. In other words, the stock is at a discount to its net present value using a higher price for gold. So if the investor's assumption is that the price of gold will one day be much higher, he or she should seek out the stock that is the most undervalued to the future gold price and not the present gold price.

The Price of Gold Stocks Relative to Their Net Present Value

In an ideal world, investors would like to buy gold stocks below their net present value and sell them above their net present value. But the investment world is far from ideal and sometimes compromises have to be made. For instance, North American gold stocks have traded at very large premiums to their net present value, in some instances as much as three to four times their net present values. These premium prices reflect the realities of investing in the gold market and the restrictions placed on some investors. Gold bullion is a commodity, and many institutional investors such as pension funds cannot hold commodities. Consequently, if such an institution wants exposure in gold, its only eligible investments are gold shares. In fact, a large part of the premium reflects this situation.

Similarly, the political climate in South Africa combined with pressures from major investors such as pension funds not to invest in that country pushed many institutions to sell their South African gold stocks and buy North American gold shares. At the same time many of the North American junior golds were unable to deliver their promised production largely because of overly optimistic views of their deposits and a lack of technical mine-building expertise. As a result, a large amount of money flooded into relatively few senior liquid gold stocks that had previously demonstrated that they had mine-building expertise. These stocks command huge valuations.

The Advantages of a Portfolio
The investor who is astute enough or lucky enough to pick one gold stock that outperforms all others will have the highest possible return. The reality of the market is that few investors can do this. While

a single stock such as American Barrick has given excellent returns, the portfolio is generally the route to go because of the benefits of diversification. Small investors can participate in portfolios using a gold mutual fund or a closed-end gold fund. A key advantage for an investor in a gold fund is liquidity.

You can sell a gold stock on the stock market, and you can sell a gold fund either on the stock market in the case of a closed-end fund or by redeeming it in the case of an open-ended fund. If the president of a gold mining company wants to sell or buy an asset, it could take months to negotiate a transaction, and even then it may not be at a favorable price. If the managers of a gold fund want to buy or sell a stock in their portfolio, then all they usually need to do is phone a broker. The transaction could be performed in hours or at the most days, and the fees charged by the stockbrokers are considerably less than the fees paid by the companies to corporate financiers when they are selling assets.

Gold funds have a major advantage for investors who cannot hold gold directly but are allowed to hold it indirectly through a fund. Moreover, fund managers can change the mix of assets in the fund to give their investors good value relative to the market as it develops.

This change of assets is extremely important because market values do change over time. For example, figure 18 shows the relationship of the share prices of the top eight North American gold pro-

Figure 18: Relative Values of Senior Gold Producers Assuming a $375 Gold Price

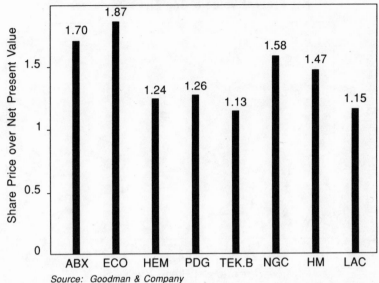

Source: Goodman & Company

ducers against their net present value as calculated using the method described earlier in this chapter.

If net present value were the sole investment criteria, the picture would not be exciting for the investor. And in fact as of mid-1992 none of the eight stocks was trading at a discount to its net present value. However, it is important to remember that net present values do not address the fact that these stocks also give the investor leverage to the gold price. Investors buy gold as insurance and because they expect that the price of gold may one day be much higher. Investors should expect to pay a premium to the net present value at today's gold price for that insurance.

Just what the insurance premium should be is

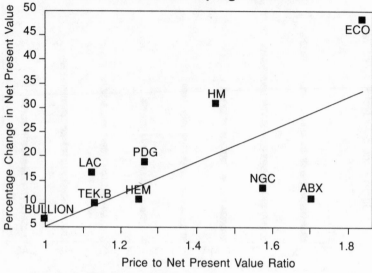

Figure 19: Impact of a $25 Gold Price Increase on Net Present Value of Top Eight Producers

Source: Goodman & Company

demonstrated in figure 19, which compares the percentage change in net present value stemming from a $25 change in the gold price, against the ratio of price to net present value. Drawing a regression line through the cluster of top producers and point (1,0) shows what the market is paying for leverage to gold price. The point (1,0) was chosen because an asset that gives the investor no leverage to the gold price should trade at its net present value. The chart shows the situation at one specific time. In reality the market is a moving target and must be constantly reviewed. Yet at the point in time the chart illustrates, four stocks appear to be relatively

Figure 20: Impact of a $25 Gold Price Increase on Net Present Value of 12 Producers

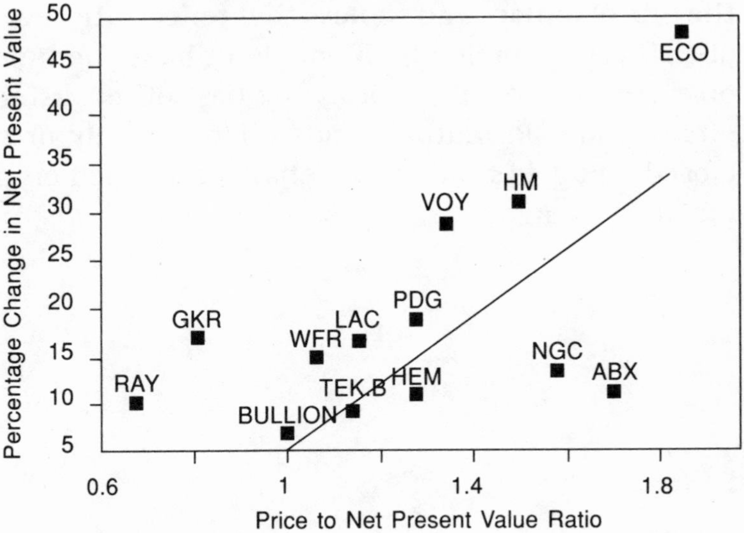

Source: Goodman & Company

good value, Lac Minerals, Placer Dome, Homestake, and Echo Bay.

Figure 20 is a modification of the previous chart and shows the addition of more junior producers. These, as the chart demonstrates, are better values. However, from an analyst's point of view, they are subject to more surprises than seniors.

Gold shares will almost certainly provide higher returns than gold bullion during the next few years as the gold price recovers. But selection is the key. If you have the time and experience to do your own analysis, you may pick the stock or handful of stocks that will be the top performers. Just remember that the odds are against you. You are probably best off creating a portfolio of gold shares, choosing the mix of juniors and seniors that reflects the level of risk you can tolerate. If you don't have the time or experience, you are probably best off choosing one of the gold mutual funds offered widely or a closed-end gold fund whose shares are listed on a major exchange.

10. How to Buy Gold Mutual Funds and Closed-end Gold Funds

Investors who want portfolios that hold gold shares, bullion, or both, but who don't want to be involved in analyzing securities and managing a portfolio, can choose professional management. Some investment counselors manage gold portfolios for clients. Also, many investment dealers can manage gold portfolios on a discretionary basis. However, to use the services of an investment counselor or to set up a managed account with a dealer, you need to have substantial assets, often exceeding hundreds of thousands of dollars. Otherwise, the portfolio won't be large enough to provide for proper diversification. As well, most counseling firms will not touch small accounts because the administrative costs can't be justified relative to the revenues generated.

Nevertheless, professional investment management is available to all gold investors through open-end gold mutual funds or closed-end gold funds. Both are investment pools whose origins date back more than a century to when the first investment pools combining the capital of many investors were established.

Using open-end gold mutual funds does not require a lot of capital. Indeed, many mutual fund companies welcome accounts with an initial purchase of as little as $1,000 or monthly accumulation plans which can be set up with monthly purchases of as little as $100. Closed-end gold funds are listed on stock exchanges and are traded like stocks. Consequently, they are available to investors with only a few thousand dollars. Moreover, the cost of professional management is minor — only about 1 percent to 3 percent annually of an open-end fund portfolio's assets. This management fee is charged to the fund. So if someone invests $10,000 in a gold mutual fund, the fee paid for professional management and administration would be about $200. There may be some acquisition or redemption costs. But these too are relatively insignificant compared to the benefits of professional management. The management fee charged to a closed-end fund is about the same as that charged to an open-end fund. In addition, a buyer of a closed-end fund would pay normal brokerage accounts for buying or selling shares.

Gold Mutual Funds

Canadian investors can choose from about 6 open-end gold mutual funds; U.S. investors can choose

from about 35. These funds combine the investments of many investors into pools, which invest
in gold securities and, depending on the specific
fund, in bullion and cash, and which are managed
by investment professionals. Investors hold shares
or units in such funds (most Canadian funds are
mutual fund trusts, which technically issue units
rather than shares). The net asset value per share
is the total value of the net assets in the fund divided by the number of shares outstanding. Such
funds are called open-end because the number of
authorized shares is unlimited and may change
from day to day as investors redeem and purchase
shares.

An investor who informs a fund before the close
of business on a given day, either directly or through
his or her broker, that he or she wishes to redeem
a specific dollar amount of a fund or a specific number of shares, will redeem at the price determined
at the close of business. At the close, the fund company calculates the value of the portfolio, using the
prices of securities supplied by stock exchanges and
gold prices supplied by major banks. The unit value
is determined by dividing the total assets by the
number of shares outstanding that day. The investor receives that price per share, less any applicable
redemption fees. Generally that money can be invested the same day in another fund managed by
the fund manager. If the investor wants cash, a
check is generally available within five business
days. Similarly, an investor who places an order to
buy shares before the close of business that same

day will pay the same price at which shares were redeemed, adjusted for any applicable acquisition fees.

To use a real example, Dynamic Precious Metals Fund had net assets of $21.9 million as of December 31, 1991, and 21.5 million units outstanding. Investors who placed orders to buy or to redeem units of the fund that day bought or redeemed at a price of $21.9 million divided by 21.5 million, or $1.02 a unit.

The main reasons for considering gold mutual funds are diversification, professional management, and liquidity.

Diversification

Diversification is a key strength of a gold mutual fund. Because investors' money is spread among many securities, there is little danger of permanent capital loss. Most funds will hold at least several dozen stocks, thus spreading risk. Should one, or even several, of the holdings in a portfolio lose most of its value because of developments affecting the company, the losses would be offset by gains in the balance of the portfolio. Since gold mining is a risky business, diversification is more important in a gold portfolio than it would be in a portfolio of senior stocks with more predictable fortunes.

Professional Management

Managing a specialized gold investment portfolio is a full-time job. Typically several people at a fund management company or investment counseling firm share responsibility for a gold portfolio. Besides the portfolio manager and securities analysts, the firm would have one or more individuals responsible for trading securities, in itself a full-time job. The portfolio manager and analysts would likely have training in geology or engineering or both, as well as business and investment training. Almost always a portfolio manager has years of experience managing investments. This is a crucial point. All the education in the world cannot replace the experience a manager gains working through several business cycles that include both rising and falling markets.

Few individuals can match the expertise of investment professionals, particularly in a specialty such as gold. Nor do they have the financial resources to make on-site inspections of a mine. Moreover, most mining companies would be extremely reluctant to allow individual investors access to a mine site. While individual investors have access to the same published material as professional investors, they rarely have access to the same flow of information from the mining industry or the investment industry or the skills necessary to evaluate technical data. This information is crucial to making informed decisions.

Liquidity
A major advantage of mutual funds is liquidity — the ability to turn an investment quickly into cash. This quality is especially important when investing in gold shares that tend to be volatile or illiquid

(lacking the ability to be turned quickly into cash). As previously noted, an individual can purchase shares of a mutual fund simply by placing his or her order with the fund company either directly or through a broker, depending on the fund. Similarly, an investor can redeem his or her shares at any time and receive the price of the fund shares for the day on which the redemption order is received. A portfolio of stocks does not offer this advantage, since some of the stocks may be "thin" traders, which do not trade in large volumes and consequently cannot be quickly liquidated. Many fund companies offer the option of switching out of a gold fund into a money market fund at no charge or for a nominal charge. Consequently, investors who want to sit on the sidelines temporarily can do so at no expense (or little expense) and almost always at less than the cost of selling a portfolio of gold shares and then buying it back.

Closed-end Funds
Closed-end gold funds are also pools of capital belonging to many investors and invested in a portfolio of gold shares and bullion managed by an investment professional. However, the number of shares outstanding is fixed in the same manner that the number of shares of a public company listed on a stock exchange is fixed. Investors who wish to buy or sell shares of such funds do not deal with the fund company. Rather, they buy or sell closed-end fund shares through a stockbroker.

This requirement can be a disadvantage because

closed-end gold fund shares tend to trade at less than the value of the underlying portfolio. In contrast, open-end funds are always redeemable at their underlying value. The discounts tend to range from zero to 30 percent, and reflect the potential illiquidity of closed-end shares. For instance, in a falling gold market there would be fewer buyers of closed-end gold funds and the discount would likely grow. Conversely, in a rising gold market with fewer sellers the discount would shrink. In fact, in times of sharply rising prices, closed-end shares could trade at a premium because of a scarcity value.

Closed-end gold funds have, however, some advantages. The fact that shares cannot be redeemed at any time gives the fund manager the option of holding less-liquid securities than the manager of an open-end gold fund. The closed-end fund manager may purchase securities as private placements — sales allowed only to institutional investors, such as mutual funds. Private placements often have restrictions on resale for specific periods, which makes them illiquid during this time.

Generally open-end mutual funds have restrictions on using borrowed money, other than to finance redemptions. Closed-end funds, depending on their specific investment policies, may borrow funds for investment purposes. The use of borrowed funds can increase a fund's return, for example if it borrowed money at an interest rate of 8 percent and invested the money in a stock that doubled in value in a year. Of course, if a portfolio partially financed with borrowed funds declines, the negative return to investors will be all that much larger because of the use of borrowed funds. Closed-end gold funds are often the choice of active stock traders.

In addition, closed-end funds can be purchased by investors worldwide. Because they trade on stock exchanges they are available through any broker-age house. A Canadian can call his or her broker to buy or sell a U.S. closed-end fund that trades on the New York Stock Exchange. Similarly, a U.S. resident can call his or her broker to buy or sell shares of a Canadian closed-end fund listed on the Toronto Stock Exchange or Montreal Exchange. In contrast, open-end mutual funds are not easily available outside the jurisdictions in which they are offered. Mutual funds may be offered only in those jurisdictions where the fund has filed its prospec-tus. Most Canadian gold mutual funds are offered in all provinces, since most funds file in all prov-inces. However, these funds are not offered in the United States. In the same vein, U.S. mutual funds are generally not available in Canada. An investor residing in Canada can write to a U.S. fund and request information about a fund and, if he or she chooses, send a check and buy that fund. Similarly, U.S. residents can request information about Ca-nadian mutual funds and make a purchase by mail. Some fund groups, however, discourage this be-cause of potential problems with securities regu-latory authorities.

Protection

Investors in both open-end and closed-end gold funds are protected if the fund manager goes out of business or has financial difficulties. The reason is that assets in a fund belong to the unit-holders or shareholders of the fund. The assets are segregated from the manager's assets and held by a custodian, generally a bank or trust company. The manager cannot use a fund's assets in its business. It cannot use the fund to purchase either its debt or its equity securities. Moreover, the fund generally cannot invest in securities of companies in which the manager is an insider. Funds are audited by independent auditors and are subject to government regulations designed to protect investors.

Selecting a Gold Fund

All gold funds perform well when gold and gold share prices are rising. Conversely, all gold funds do poorly when gold and gold share prices are falling. The key determinant in the performance of a gold fund is the direction and magnitude of gold and gold share prices. However, relative performance of gold funds depends on a number of factors — the skills of the fund manager, investment restrictions of the fund, and the general philosophy of the fund.

While all gold funds invest in gold and gold-backed assets, there are subtle differences in investment philosophy and strategy that investors should consider before making their choice. The information needed is included in the fund prospectus and in annual and quarterly reports issued by the fund.

The prospectus is a legal document that offers the fund to investors and includes the basic information about a fund that an investor needs in order to make a decision. The prospectus is available from the fund and from brokers and fund dealers who sell the fund. It includes information about fees and other expenses and details the investment philosophy, noting any important investment restrictions. It also notes any privileges investors have, such as no-cost or low-cost transfers into other funds managed by the same fund management company.

Look at the Portfolio
It is important that investors obtain copies of a fund's annual and quarterly reports. These contain the fund's financial statements, in particular the statements of investments or portfolios. By examining these, investors can determine the fund's holdings and much about its philosophy. Comparing statements of consecutive periods, investors can see what portfolio changes the fund manager has made. The annual and interim statements include commentaries on the market and current investment strategy. These give some insight as to what course of action the manager is currently taking.

Examining the prospectus, annual and interim reports, and sales literature or dealers' commentaries, investors will quickly discover that some funds invest only in gold and gold securities. While all precious-metals funds emphasize gold or gold shares as their primary investments, some may include silver, platinum, and palladium as well as shares of producers of these precious metals. Some funds may have geographical restrictions on their investments. For instance, most Canadian mutual funds concentrate on Canadian gold shares and bullion so that the funds can be eligible for government-approved retirement savings programs called registered retirement savings plans. A fund may have a restriction that prohibits any investment in South African gold mining companies. Others are free to invest in all markets or may be geared to invest in specific overseas markets.

The material available will also disclose any constraints on the assets a fund may hold. For example, a fund may vary its asset mix between bullion and shares. However, the manager may be required to hold a minimum position in bullion at all times, based on percentage of assets. Another fund may have no such restriction, effectively allowing its manager to hold any mix of bullion and shares it believes reasonable given expected market conditions.

A fund may take the view that its investors want the fund always fully invested in gold and that those investors who are worried about the gold market will redeem. Consequently, that fund will hold only enough cash to meet anticipated redemptions. Another fund manager will hold the view that its investors are taking a long-term view of the market and want the manager to take a fully managed approach. That manager will vary the mix of gold bullion, gold shares, and cash to reflect expected market conditions. Such a fund might place a major portion of the portfolio in treasury bills if the manager expected gold prices to decline.

Different managers will have different policies towards the size of companies in the portfolio. For example, a manager may decide to hold the majority of assets in shares of senior gold producers. Another manager may aim at medium-size companies that it believes have the best potential for gain. Yet another manager may build a portfolio of junior gold companies with the potential to become producers. In some markets these will outperform all other gold funds and, conversely, underperform all other funds when juniors are out of favor.

Look at the Manager

To be in the fund management business, a company must meet specific minimum financial requirements, and the key people who are responsible for the management of portfolios must meet specific minimum educational and experience requirements. Nevertheless, some managers have better qualifications than others, and it is up to investors or their advisers to determine who has what. This information is often obtainable from fund sales literature. If it is not available in this material, it is almost certainly available from the fund company.

It is important to consider the manager's education, experience, and investment philosophy. The portfolio manager and senior analysts should have specialized education in investments. Generally, each would have an M.B.A. or Chartered Financial

Analyst designation or similar degree or certificate. In addition, those members of the management company with responsibilities involving gold stocks should have specialized training such as a degree in geology, geological engineering, or mining engineering or the equivalent experience from working in the mining industry.

It is also important to determine how a company researches its investments. Economic data and world gold supply and demand figures can be examined from behind a desk, of course. Similarly, an analyst doesn't have to leave his or her office to review annual reports and other information released by a mining company. However, there is much more to analyzing gold companies than reading reports and making models on a computer. Analysts can learn much by making inspections of mine sites, speaking with geologists and others working in the field, and above all meeting with the management of mine companies. Analysts and portfolio managers aren't going to be given inside information. They will, however, come away with a better understanding of the project, which will be reflected in their recommendations to buy, sell, continue to hold, or avoid shares of a specific company.

Look at Performance
The reason for holding a gold mutual fund or closed-end gold fund is, for most investors, to get a return superior to the one they would get by holding gold bullion alone. With this objective in mind, investors

should compare a fund's performance against returns from holding gold bullion. To do this, they
should use one or more of the major fund performance tables published in the U.S. and Canadian
business press. Most brokers can provide performance information on closed-end funds, the same
way they provide performance information on individual stocks.

The difficulty, however, in choosing a fund on the
basis of its performance is that most funds have
not been in existence for more than a few years.
As well, the volatility of the gold markets through
most of the 1980s makes judgments on the basis
of performance difficult. The credentials of the
manager should therefore be given at least the same
weighting, if not a heavier weighting, as past performance in making the decision about what fund
to buy.

Look at Costs
All gold mutual funds charge a management fee,
which ranges from about 1 to 3 percent of the fund
assets annually and which generally is charged to
the fund monthly. All funds pay their manager out
of this fee. Some absorb all of the fund's expenses
out of this fee as well, excluding brokerage costs
and taxes, if any. Other funds charge fund expenses such as the cost of producing annual and
corporate reports to the fund. The actual expenses
an investor pays may therefore be higher than the
management fee.

To allow investors to make valid comparisons of

costs, securities regulators require all funds to report a management expense ratio, which shows the true cost of the fund. This figure is included in the fund prospectus or annual report and is reported in several of the performance surveys. The management expense ratios of gold mutual funds range from about 1 percent to more than 3 percent. Most investors do not consider the differences in management expense ratios significant when funds produce high returns. But when the market marks time or declines, small differences are significant.

Investors must also consider acquisition or redemption fees. Funds that are sold directly to investors by a fund management company and that charge no acquisition fees are called "no-load" funds. Investors who buy these pay no sales charges or acquisition fees (unless they redeem within a short time, in which case they would pay a small redemption fee). The majority of gold funds, however, are sold through stockbrokers and mutual fund dealers who are paid a sales commission. There are three types of sales charges: acquisition fees, which are paid when fund shares are purchased; redemption fees, which are paid when fund shares are redeemed; and ongoing charges for marketing, which are charged against the fund monthly. Some funds are offered only with acquisition fees. Others give the investor the option of choosing either an acquisition fee or a redemption fee.

U.S. load funds charge acquisition fees of up to 8.5 percent of the money invested, though many charge less than this maximum. An investor plac-

ing $10,000 in a fund with an 8.5 percent com-
mission rate would pay $850 commission and have
$9,150 invested in the fund.

Canadian load funds charge acquisition fees of
up to 9 percent, but these decline with the size of
an order. A typical fund commission schedule would
state a maximum charge of 9 percent for purchases
of up to $15,000, 8 percent for purchases of $15,000
to $25,000, and so on. So an investor who decided
to invest $10,000 in a fund would pay up to $900
as an acquisition fee, leaving $9,100 for the pur-
chase of fund shares. These fees, however, are
maximums and are discounted by many brokers.
Discount brokers, in fact, charge half the posted
maximum rate. As well, many full service dealers
will discount mutual fund commissions to be competitive with discount brokers.

Many fund companies on both sides of the border
have switched to redemption fees or offer redemption fees as an alternative to acquisition fees. The
fund company pays the selling broker or dealer a
sales commission, which it hopes to recover from
management fees over time or out of redemption
fees if the investor withdraws from the fund within
a few years. The "contingent declining" redemption fees generally decline over time so that long-
term investors in a fund will not pay any redemption fee. A typical redemption fee would be 4.5 percent of the value of assets withdrawn if an investor
redeems within one year of purchase. The rates
would decline by half a percentage point each year,
so that someone who holds a fund for eight years

would pay no redemption fee. Redemption fees are generally calculated on the value of shares redeemed rather than the purchase price. However, shares purchased from reinvested dividend distributions are generally exempt from redemption fees, and fund companies look at these as being the first shares redeemed. Similarly, shares held longest are considered the first to be redeemed, again reducing the cost to investors.

Some U.S. funds with redemption fees also have what are called 12b-1 charges, which are generally around 0.5 percent but in some cases exceed 1 percent. Their purpose is to fund the commission paid to the broker. In Canada this type of charge is rare. However, several major fund companies have raised management fees substantially in recent years to reflect the jump in marketing costs stemming from the move to redemption fees from acquisition fees.

Long-term investors are better off choosing a redemption fee over an acquisition fee because with a redemption fee all their money is invested in the fund and because they will avoid any fees if they hold long enough. This advantage holds only if the management fee charged when the fund is sold with a redemption fee is no higher than when the fund is sold with an acquisition fee.

Of course, costs are an important part of selecting a fund, and no-load funds — funds sold without any acquisition or redemption fees — have a distinctive advantage.

In Canada someone investing a very large amount may be able to negotiate an acquisition fee as low as a fraction of percentage point cent on orders of $100,000 or more. Once paid, that investor has the flexibility to move out without triggering additional costs.

Investors who plan to trade in and out of the market should look closely at their potential costs before choosing a fund. Canadian investors considering a fund that is available with either an acquisition fee or redemption fee should try to negotiate an acquisition fee lower than the first year's redemption fee. This will cut their trading costs, assuming they redeem within the first year.

Because gold funds are extremely volatile and investors may want to move to the sidelines temporarily, it makes sense to determine if the fund company being considered offers a money market fund to which an investor can move without paying a redemption fee or additional acquisition fees. Some fund groups give their clients this option. A redemption fee would be paid only if the client redeemed the shares of the second fund and moved the money out. In such a case the redemption fee would be calculated based on when the funds were first invested within the group.

Choosing a Broker

Those investors who do not deal directly with a fund company will need a broker or fund dealer to execute their orders. This decision is less crucial for people who do their own research. However, if you want to deal with a broker who can provide you with advice on gold, deal only with a specialist or someone who has access to specialized advice.

Determine the broker's experience and knowledge. It is important to find someone whose advice has some substance rather than a person who parrots an article from that day's business pages. Does the broker have access to research analysts with substantial experience in gold mining or to the fund company's managers? Is the broker willing to spend the time necessary to research answers to your questions? Whether he or she will, of course, often depends on how often you ask questions, the size of your account, and how often you trade. Finally, will the broker keep you up to date about developments in your funds without being prodded? Often fund companies send brokers information that they don't send to individual clients, or hold meetings with fund managers to brief brokers on developments and trends.

Strategies
Accumulation Plans

Most mutual fund management companies offer purchase plans to encourage ongoing investments in their funds and to encourage small investors to accumulate additional shares. These accumulation plans are called dollar-cost-averaging plans, automatic purchase plans, or preauthorized purchase plans, and they allow investors to buy specific dollar amounts of a fund each month or quarter. An investor decides how much of a gold fund he or she wishes to purchase each month. He or she then fills out an account form, authorizing the investor's bank to pay that amount to the fund company each month, and supplies the fund company with a check marked "void." Each month, on a specific date, the money will be withdrawn from the investor's account and used to purchase shares of the chosen gold fund.

Such accumulation plans have several advantages for an investor. They allow the investor to accumulate capital. They allow the investor to avoid trying to pick the best times to buy gold funds. In periods of falling markets, an investor's monthly purchase will buy more shares, lowering an investor's average cost. Of course, during rising markets, an investor will buy fewer shares and raise his or her average cost. Nevertheless, such a plan works well for long-term investors. The minimum required to open an account is generally $100 a month, and the amount can be varied by giving written notice to the fund company. An investor can terminate the arrangement at any time by giving the fund company notice in writing. Similarly, the plan can be put on hold temporarily.

Figure 21 shows how an investor would have fared if he or she had set up a monthly accumulation plan with $100 a month over the five years ended December 31, 1991. The calculation uses month-end unit values of Dynamic Precious Metals Fund and of its predecessor, Dynamic-Guardian Gold Fund. The figures ignore acquisition and redemption fees, which would have been applicable

Figure 21: Growth of $100 a Month Invested in a Gold Mutual Fund over 72 Months ending December 31, 1991

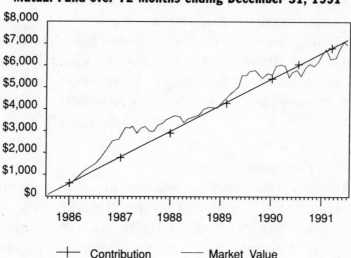

—+— Contribution   —— Market Value

to some investors. It ignores the effect of any income taxes for which the investor might be responsible.

Withdrawal Plans
The mirror image of an accumulation plan is a withdrawal plan in which an individual invests a lump sum in a gold fund and withdraws a specific amount each month. The minimum amount for setting up a withdrawal plan varies from fund to fund, but the range is $5,000 to $15,000. As a result withdrawal plans are feasible for investors who are using their capital for income and who want to put 5 to 15 percent of their assets into gold. Fund companies that offer funds with redemption fees often

have provisions that allow investors to withdraw up to 10 percent of the value of the plan each year without triggering any redemption fees.

Figure 22 simulates a withdrawal plan based on $100,000 invested in Dynamic Precious Metals Fund on January 1, 1987. The simulation ignores any applicable acquisition or redemption fees and taxes.

Using Borrowed Funds

Many investors use borrowed money to buy investments in the expectation that the additional return they will earn will more than offset interest costs and increase their return on their own capital. However, using borrowed capital increases risk.

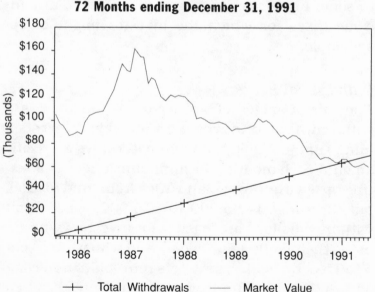

Figure 22: $1,000 a Month Withdrawal Plan over 72 Months ending December 31, 1991

+ Total Withdrawals   — Market Value

As we have noted, a key investment objective for everyone is preservation of capital. Using borrowed capital to buy gold investment funds is contrary to that objective if a paper loss results in a loan being called and forces an investor to liquidate his or her investment, resulting in a permanent capital loss. So the first rule about using borrowed capital to buy a gold investment fund is: don't if you have limited capital and could be forced into a position of having to sell your investment. If, however, you have a diversified portfolio, purchased with your own capital, and decide to use a fraction as collateral to increase holdings of gold funds, then using borrowed funds or leverage is a consideration.

Using borrowed funds has not been profitable for investors in gold funds over the past several years because the overall returns have not exceeded the cost of capital. Investors would have been better off not borrowing and using the money that otherwise would have been used to pay interest to buy additional fund shares. However, leverage is a consideration for investors who believe that gold prices will surge over the next several years and provide substantial returns exceeding those available from using their own capital.

Leverage makes sense only if you expect to make substantially above-average returns over a short period and if you have enough financial strength to ride out any temporary declines in the market. In other words, you should avoid using borrowed funds if you can be forced into liquidating your investments, realizing permanent losses.

11. Options and Futures

Just two decades ago investors who wanted to trade in gold had basically two choices: they could deal in the metal — bullion or coins — or they could buy and sell shares of gold producers. That changed in the early 1970s when the Winnipeg Exchange introduced the first 400-ounce gold futures contract in response to the decision of central bankers to no longer keep the price of gold at $35 an ounce and, instead, allow it float. In 1974 the U.S. government repealed the law that prevented U.S. citizens from owning gold, and in December 1974 Comex (the New York Commodity Exchange) introduced its first gold futures contracts. Then in the early 1980s several exchanges in Canada, the United States, Europe, Australia, and the Far East introduced gold options contracts. Today, the value of trading in these "derivatives" exceeds the value of trading in physical gold.

Investors can also trade options on shares of some of the major gold producers, including Lac Minerals, International Corona, and Placer Dome, through the Trans Canada Options Inc., the clearing corporation owned by the major Canadian exchanges, and on shares of several U.S. gold producers, including Homestake and Newmont. You can even trade in options on the Philadelphia Exchange's Gold/Silver index. In addition to these exchange-traded derivatives, there is substantial over-the-counter market in options involving mining companies and major gold dealers. Gold loans are another derivative.

The derivative markets are very important to the gold markets. They allow producers to hedge against wide price movements. They also provide a means for individual investors and even central banks to hedge positions against price movements and for speculators to have the opportunity to make large gains or losses. Options can also be used to provide income from a bullion holding. Moreover, derivatives provide liquidity to the marketplace and can influence the spot price.

Gold futures
A gold futures contract is an agreement to deliver or accept delivery of a specific amount of gold at a specified date at a firm price agreed upon at the time the agreement was made. Let's use the Comex contract as an example. The size of each Comex contract is 100 ounces for delivery in a specified month. You can trade contracts for delivery during

the current calendar month; the next two calendar months; and February, April, June, August, October, and December falling within a 23-month period beginning with the current month. The purpose for limiting the number of delivery months is to concentrate trading to improve liquidity. A liquid market helps prevent distortions. Contracts can trade every day up to and including the third-last business day of the maturing delivery month.

The price of a futures contract is tied to the spot price, with the spread between the spot price and futures price increasing with the distance to delivery month. So the difference between a December 1993 contract and the spot price in February 1992 would be higher than the spread between a June 1992 contract and the February 1992 spot price. The difference in price is called the "contango." Gold is normally in a contango market in which the price of the futures contract is higher than the spot price. Because gold supplies are normally available for financial transactions — gold can almost always be borrowed from an investment dealer (the actual lender might be a central bank, which is paid interest), if necessary, for delivery — the contango consists primarily of the interest charges that would be necessary to finance carrying gold until the delivery month along with storage and insurance costs. The contango almost always equals the carrying costs of gold over the period to delivery date. If it gets out of line, say, rising above the cost of carrying gold, bullion dealers and other "arbitrageurs" (who make money trying to benefit from price differences in markets) would sell the futures contract and buy bullion to earn the difference between the contango and the actual cost of carrying gold.

Several commodity exchanges in North America trade gold futures. However, trading volumes on the Comex dwarf trading on the others, including the Chicago Board of Trade and the Mid-America Exchange. The CBOT has a 1-kilogram contract in addition to its 100-ounce contract. The smaller contract tends to attract smaller speculators. The Chicago Mercantile Exchange ceased trading its gold contract in 1988.

Contracts are traded overseas in a number of markets, including Hong Kong, Sydney, and Tokyo. The Tokyo Commodity Exchange is the most significant overseas exchange. While trading activity has been growing, the trading volume of its 1-kilogram contracts, in equivalent weight of gold, is less than 10 percent of Comex volume.

Prices of gold futures contracts can be found in tables in any financial newspaper. The tables show, for each delivery month, the opening price of the contract, its high and low price for the day, its closing price, the change on the day, and the open interest — the number of contracts outstanding at the close of the day. The tables also show the estimated number of trades during the day, the previous day's trading volume, and the total open interest.

The contract is marketable, and only a small percentage of contracts are actually delivered. Generally buyers and sellers close their positions before expiry date by buying or selling offsetting positions. For instance, a speculator who bought a futures contract for delivery in, say, December 1991, wouldn't take delivery of the gold. Rather, he or she would sell a December 1991 contract before the delivery date. Futures are used by gold producers to hedge against price movements in the market. For example, a gold mining company that wants to lock in a certain amount of revenues for gold it will be producing over the next year would sell contracts, locking in a specific price. That way its cash flow would be immune to any drop in the price of gold. Similarly, a jewelry manufacturer that has to quote a firm price to customers would use the futures market to lock in a price for the gold it will need in advance. When it needs the gold, it will likely buy in the spot market and sell the contract. If the price of gold goes up, its profit on the futures contract would offset the higher price it would pay for gold. Conversely, if the price of gold declines, it would take a loss on each contract, but this would be offset by the lower price it would pay for gold. So no matter which way gold moves, its margins from manufacturing would not change.

Whereas producers and gold users use futures for hedging, many individuals use futures for speculating on the direction of the price of gold. Futures contracts are useful for speculators because they don't have to own gold or take delivery. Moreover, they have to put up a only portion of the value of the contract as margin or good faith money, generally a few thousand dollars per contract. For example, someone who wants to buy 10 contracts would in effect be agreeing to accept delivery of 1,000 ounces of gold. The value of 10 December 1992 contracts purchased on February 8, 1991, would be $404,700. Assuming the dealer requires a margin of 10 percent, that individual would have to tie up only about $40,000 of capital.

If the price of the gold moves up 10 percent, that person would in effect double his investment before commissions. The increase in price of the contract or paper profit gives the investor additional margin to buy another contract and "pyramid" his holdings. This practice can, however, prove risky because of gold's volatility. The leverage provided by futures contracts can work two ways, and goes against this investor if the price drops. A decline of 10 percent in the price of gold after that investor's initial purchase would wipe out that investor's initial margin deposit.

If the price declines, an investor is required to put up additional margin immediately. If he cannot, the broker is required to liquidate the position. Indeed, most brokers require clients to keep an adequate margin cushion with the brokerage firm, usually in the form of U.S. treasury bills.

An investor who expects the price of gold to decline could sell a futures contract. In this case, the profit would be the decline in the value of the contract, less commission. If the price rises in this case, the investor would be required to put up additional margin.

Futures trading is obviously not for everyone. Generally, dealers will open accounts only for people who have the financial assets and income level that indicate they can afford the risks of futures trading. Fortunes have and will continue to be made trading gold futures contracts. Yet many people have lost fortunes when the markets have moved against them.

Investors can use many techniques to reduce their risk. They can put in "stop loss" orders, in which their brokers are given instructions to eliminate their positions if the price hits a specified level. However, this protection is far from automatic, and a sharp move in the price could take place without the execution of their trade. The futures exchanges have rules that prevent abnormally large moves in price by setting a "limit" to the move allowed in any given day — $25. If the change in settlement price moves the limit for two consecutive days, an expanded limit is automatically introduced. Limits, however, don't apply to prices for the current delivery or spot month. Many traders use more than one contract to reduce their risk.

Options

Unlike gold futures contracts, which are obligations to deliver or receive bullion, gold options give investors the "right" to buy or sell gold at a specific price up to a specific date. Options are traded on exchanges around the world. The most active market is the Comex, in which the gold option is based on the Comex gold futures contract rather than on bullion. Gold options are also traded on the Montreal Exchange, the Vancouver Stock Exchange, the European Options Exchange in Amsterdam, the Sydney Stock Exchange (these "International Options Clearing Corporation" options are interchangeable, giving investors an $18^1/_2$ hour trading day), the Mid-America Exchange, and the Bolsa Mercantil & de Futuros in São Paulo. In all cases an exchange clearing corporation guarantees that obligations stemming from options contracts are fulfilled. Tables showing options trading are published daily in the business press.

The Comex options contract is tied to the Comex 100-ounce futures contract. The Mid-America contract is for 33.2 ounces, while the BM&F contract is for 250 grams of gold. The IOCC contracts cover 10 ounces of gold.

There are two types of options. A "call" option gives the holder the right to buy gold at a fixed price, the "exercise" or "strike" price, up to a specified expiry date. A "put" option gives the holder the right to sell gold at a fixed exercise price up to the expiry date. The buyer of the option pays what is called a "premium" to the seller of the option for this right. The premium may have an "intrinsic value," which is the amount by which the price of the option is above the price of gold in the case of a call option and below the price of gold in the case of a put option. An option that has an intrinsic value is "in-the-money." An option that has no intrinsic value is "out-of-the-money." If the strike price and gold price are the same, the option is "at-the-money." The price of an option is almost always equal to or greater than its intrinsic value. If it was traded below its intrinsic value, the difference would quickly disappear because arbitrageurs would buy and exercise the options while selling or buying gold or a gold futures contract, taking the difference less transaction costs as profit.

The difference between the premium and intrinsic value is the "time value" of the option. It reflects the additional amount investors are willing to pay for the expectation that the option will increase in value before its expiration date. Usually the time value of an option decreases as the expiry date approaches. Options that are deeply out-of-the-money are likely to have a substantially lower time value than options that are only slightly out-of-the-money or in-the-money with the same expiry date because the deeply out-of-the-money options are less likely to be exercised before the expiry date. Figure 23 shows call option values two months before expiry and at expiry.

While the holder of the option will exercise the option only if it is to his or her financial advantage, the seller or option "writer" is obligated to sell gold at the exercise price in the case of a call option or buy gold in the case of the put option at any time before the expiry date. If an option is not exercised, it expires worthless.

The size of the premium depends on the actual price of gold, the strike price of the option, the length of time before the option expires, and the anticipated volatility in the price of gold. All these vari-

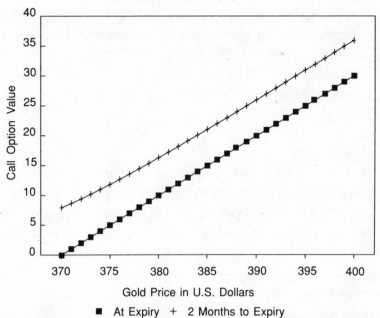

Figure 23: Gold Call Option Values
Before and at Expiry

Gold Price in U.S. Dollars

■ At Expiry   + 2 Months to Expiry

Source: Nesbitt Thomson Inc.

ables are known except the anticipated volatility of the market. Market makers will price options using a formula based on what is called the Black-Scholes model, or some modification. Indeed, most dealers use computer programs that can provide their clients with calculations of potential profits using assumptions about where the price of gold may move.

Options are less risky than futures, but they can still be risky. While the maximum loss an investor can expect is the price of the premium plus commission, options can and often do expire worthless.

Consequently, a speculator can lose all of his or her capital. Conversely, because the premiums are generally only a fraction of the value of the strike price, options can offer speculators very large profits based on movements in the price of gold. Investors dealing in options should not overlook the cost of commissions and should obtain schedules from their brokers.

Some Examples
How you use options depends on how you expect the price of gold to move and whether your objective is to hedge or to speculate. Often the same strategies can be used by both hedgers and speculators.

First, let's take the case of an individual who expects the price of gold to rise over the next few months but who wants to make a larger profit per dollar of capital than someone who would hold gold outright. This individual might buy a call option. Say the price of gold is $370 an ounce in February, and a June $370 call option can be purchased at a premium of $14 an ounce. If the price of gold rises to, say, $400 before the expiry date, the price of that option will at least double. The actual profit will depend on how soon the price of gold rises. If gold moves to $400 in March, the premium will be at least $30 — the intrinsic value — plus some time value reflecting the fact that the expiry date is still several months away. The holder of the option could sell the option, taking a profit, or continue to hold in the hope that the price will rise even higher. Alternatively, the investor could sell and purchase another option with an expiry date further into the future. Figure 24 shows the range of potential profit or loss at expiry for this transaction.

This same strategy would be used by someone who wants to buy gold but limit the potential loss should the price decline. Rather than buying bullion, he buys options contracts, which, if exercised, would give the amount of gold he would otherwise buy. The potential loss is limited to the cost of the premium. The flip side of the coin is that his potential profits are also reduced by the cost of the premium.

A second case might involve an individual who expects the price of gold to fall. She could sell a

Figure 24: Gold Call Option

Profit/Loss at Expiry

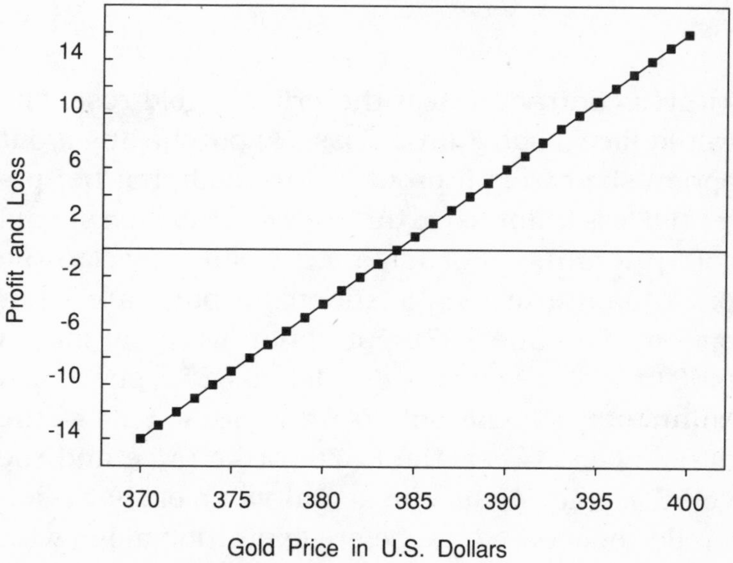

Gold Price in U.S. Dollars

Source: Nesbitt Thomson Inc.

Figure 25: Gold Put Option
Profit/Loss at Expiry

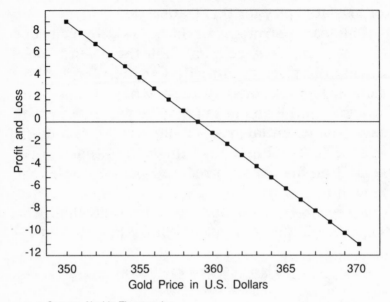

Source: Nesbitt Thomson Inc.

futures contract. But if the price of gold rose, she would face a substantial loss. By purchasing a put option she can still profit if prices fall, but her potential loss is limited to the price of the option should gold prices rise. For instance, if she expected the price to fall from $370, she might purchase a put option. If a June $370 put option were purchased for $11 and the price of gold fell to $350, she would be able to sell the option for at least $20 — the difference between the $370 strike price and the value of gold. Again the actual value of the option would reflect the time before expiration along with market expectations as to how low gold will go. Figure 25 shows the potential range of profit or loss at expiry of this transaction.

Call and put options can also be purchased as part of a trading strategy. An individual with a substantial gold holding may be nervous about the short-term outlook for gold. He could sell his position, locking in his profit, and take part of his profit to buy options. That way, if the price rises, he can repurchase his position by exercising his option. He could accomplish the same objective by continuing to hold his position and buying put options. If the price of gold rises, his holding continues to appreciate. But if the price declines, his loss would be offset by the appreciation of the put options contracts, which he could sell. The decision to sell his holding and buy call options or, alternatively, to maintain his position and buy put options depends on the price of the options and whether he might face tax liabilities if he sold his gold holding. In these cases, the cost of the option is a form of insurance.

An investor who holds gold can hedge by writing gold call options. As the writer of the call option, she receives the premium and earns income on her gold position. Assume that the price of gold is $370 in February, the price of a June $380 call option is $9, and our investor feels that gold is likely to stay at about $370 for the next few months at least. By writing call options she will receive the premium of $9 an ounce. If the price of bullion remains at $370 or does not rise above $380, she will earn a profit of $9 an ounce and maintain her position. If the price declines, she has the premium to offset the decline. But if the price rises above $380, the option will be exercised. That wouldn't necessarily be bad news. She would receive that $380 per ounce price and have the premium as well. Figure 26 shows the potential profit or loss from writing this option.

Most investors who write call options own bullion, certificates, or gold futures contracts and do so to earn income. Their activity is called "covered writing." Investors who write calls without owning calls are required to put up substantial margin to reflect the fact that, in theory, there is no limit to

Figure 26: Gold Call Option Covered Writing
Profit and Loss

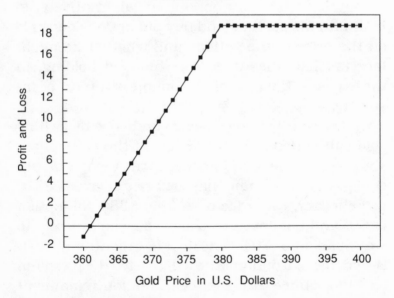

Source: Nesbitt Thomson Inc.

their liability. Required margin is about 10 percent of the contract's underlying market, less the out-of-the-money value or plus the premium.

Someone who wants to buy gold but believes the price is too high can try a different tack — writing put options. Using once again a market price of $370 an ounce for gold, this person could write a June $360 put option and receive a premium of about $7 an ounce. If the price of gold declined to $360 or less, the option would be exercised and he would be required to buy gold at $360 an ounce. His actual cost would be offset by the fact that he received a premium for assuming the obligation to buy gold at $360 an ounce. However, if the price of gold were sharply lower than the exercise price, the premium would not be enough to offset his losses. Our investor could, of course, cancel his obligation before the expiry date by purchasing a June $370 put option. Figure 27 shows the potential profit or loss from writing a put option.

As with futures contracts, options traders employ strategies using more than one contract to reduce their risk or cut their costs. For example, an investor who expects the price of gold to decline can purchase one put and sell another, reducing the cost but lowering her potential profit as well. If June $370 puts are trading at $11 and June $360 puts are trading at $6, she could buy $370 puts and sell $360 puts for a net cost of $5. The act of selling one option against another is known as "spreading." In this case, since the strategy will profit if gold falls in value, it is known as "bear spreading."

Figure 27: Put Write
Profit and Loss

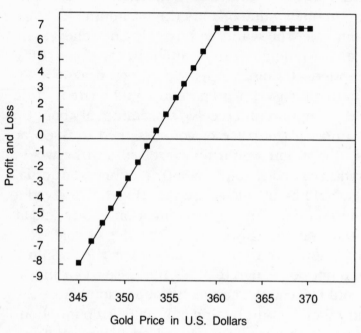

Source: Nesbitt Thomson Inc.

In return for a lower cost she also gives up potential profit. The most the strategy can return is the difference between the two exercise prices of the put options less the cost of establishing the spread. If gold fell to $350, the June $360 put would be repurchased for $10 and the June $370 call would be sold for $20. Applying the initial cost of $5 against the resulting $10 credit gives a $5 profit. Figure 28 shows the potential profit and loss from a gold option bear spread.

Figure 28: Gold Option Bear Spread
Profit and Loss

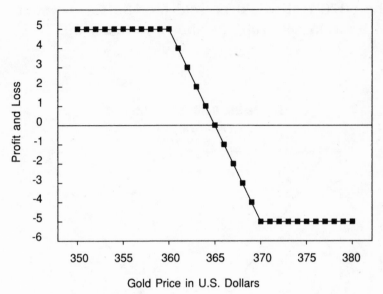

Gold Price in U.S. Dollars

Source: Nesbitt Thomson Inc.

Another investor may simply anticipate an increase in volatility and a large price swing in one direction or another. Since he is indifferent to the direction of the price move, he will purchase both a call and a put. This strategy is known as a "straddle." If gold is trading at $370 and June $370 puts are trading at $11 and June $370 calls are trading are $14, then to purchase both will cost $25. As can be seen from the large cost of the transaction, this person anticipates quite a move in the price of gold. If by June gold fell to $330, then the $370 call would expire worthless and the $370 put would be sold for $40 for a total net profit of $15. If gold rose to $400, then the put would expire worthless and the $370 call would be sold for $30. This would mean a $5 net profit, as shown in figure 29.

Figure 29: Gold Option Straddle

Profit and Loss

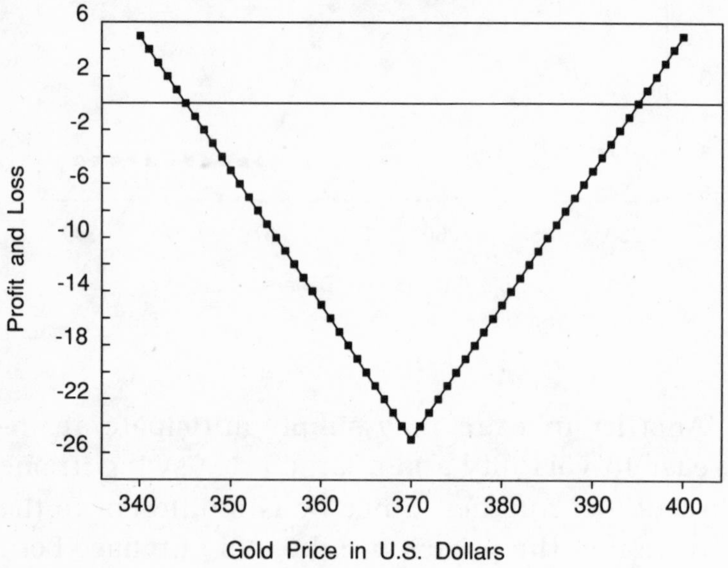

Gold Price in U.S. Dollars

Source: Nesbitt Thomson Inc.

12. The Outlook for Gold

In the preceding pages, we have argued that the price of gold tracks the worldwide rate of inflation, not always precisely, either in momentum or degree, but inevitably. Our view on forecasting is that it is always better to know the right direction than the precise timing. Clearly, from the current perspective of one sitting in North America, the future for inflation as measured by the consumer price index and as driven by the money supply, is higher and not lower. Our North American–style democratic system requires that politicians cater to the electorate in order to be reelected. Recessions, depressions, and periods of deflation are all harbingers of the demise of a political career.

Most of the successful political regimes in our democratic society have been fed by small doses of inflation in order to provide the electorate with the goodies that they believe belong to them by right.

Furthermore, we have developed a population which is predominantly middle-class and which has as its number-one desire the ownership of a personal dwelling. Small doses of inflation have always been greeted with a cheer by owners of small pieces of real estate. Today, even the burgeoning senior citizen population enters that category owning real estate. Any politician worth his or her salt soon learns that inflation gets him or her reelected and deflation, depression and recession send him or her in search of an alternative career.

Inflation is driven by money supply. Politicians in power can control money supply. We are entering an era in the 1990s during which massive reflationary efforts are required in order to provide jobs, build roads, provide social services such as health care, help the former Eastern bloc countries to develop democratic institutions, and stave off outright deflation and depression. We have faith that our politicians have sufficient intelligence to recognize this fact. The money supply will be increased and higher rates of inflation, believe it or not, will be received by the populace with relief because inflation serves to create employment and social services, and bring confidence back to the North American consumer. These inflationary forces will emerge quietly and timidly at first, but will eventually create problems at increasing rates as the rest of this decade unfolds.

The massive debt structures of Canada and the United States will have to be monetized before the end of this decade. The last round of debt monetization in North America occurred just prior to the 1970s. It led to double-digit inflation accompanied by runaway rates of interest, and, coincidentally, to a runaway gold price in 1979 and 1980. At that time, key members of what now is called the G7 group of countries, notably Germany and Japan, had perfect control over their money supply, as well as their rates of inflation. The monetization of debt that occurred in the early 1970s was a North American phenomenon.

Today, the former Soviet bloc of countries all are experiencing unbelievably high rates of inflation as they catch up after 70 years of fixed prices under socialism. Germany is just beginning to realize that the costs of unification will be well in excess of their worst fears and that they have very limited ability to curtail money supply increases in order to comfortably integrate two economies. Japan, to stop itself from totally sinking into the Pacific, must reflate or go into a depression that could have international consequences. And of course we know the story about North America's enormous, continuing governmental deficit, financing practices and buildup of government debt into the trillions of dollars.

With a U.S. dollar that is undervalued when compared with the Deutschmark or the French franc, we fully expect that inflation rates during the 1990s will average around 6 to 7 percent in the United States. When you consider that we are already through two years of rates of inflation well below that average, you can see that we expect much higher rates of inflation in the immediate years to come.

In a recent private publication, our former partner and fellow gold aficionado, Pierre Lassonde, wrote: "In fact, society in general views deflation with attendant high unemployment, as chaos that ultimately leads to revolutions." There is no doubt that the recent events in the former Soviet Union are in the minds of the public and elected officials alike. Hyperinflation is no better, of course, as it leads right down the same path. So what are we left with? By leaning to the side of prudence, we come to see a little inflation as the least of all evils. A little inflation, — anything below double-digit numbers — is seen today as a social stabilizer. Inflation becomes the lubricant that governments use to keep the system from overheating. Without an anchor, such as the gold standard, there is no way to tell how long our society can postpone its day of reckoning. We suspect it will take a lot longer than generally perceived.

The most important function served by gold over the course of some 6,000 years — far more important than its transformation into trinkets, coins and seemingly frivolous items — has been its use as a counter to the inflationary forces that depreciate the currency of the day. As the 1990s unfold and inflation rather than deflation, or the lack of inflation, becomes the topic of the day, gold will once again take on its traditional role.

This will come at a time when gold production worldwide has peaked. All our studies indicate that the production of newly mined gold will be in decline from mid-1992 into the foreseeable future, or at least until there is a significant upward adjustment to the price. The lack of exploration by mining companies, the fierceness of environmental laws, the discovery of very few ore bodies in the recent past, and simply the lower grades of ore in mines that are currently producing, all lead to the conclusion that gold production on a global basis should begin to decline.

Moreover, the rewriting of world gold production statistics to reflect Soviet sales from gold reserves rather than production will increase the perception of declining supply. Similarly the impact of forward selling on supply will diminish as producers begin to deliver the gold that was sold several years earlier.

The country that produces most gold, South Africa, is going into a period in its political cycle which, at the very least, could provide some disruptive moments to the world supply of gold. More important, South Africa under its new regime will be obliged to provide higher wages to its mine workers. To achieve this without inflation and still remain profitable, the industry will produce gold from its higher-grade ores using fewer people. This means lower gold supply from South Africa and a quicker depletion of ore reserves.

Even during the recession and a bear market for gold, the demand for gold jewelry in Europe and especially Asia has been growing dramatically, reflecting increasing wealth.

All this is occurring at a time when central bank and investment demand for gold as a monetary reserve is in decline. Several central banks have taken a short-term solution to their problems of deficits and lack of fiscal discipline by selling gold into the open market. The former Soviet Union was technically bankrupt before it sold all its gold reserve.

The Canadian central bank appears to be following the path of the former Soviet Union, while vibrant countries such as Taiwan and Spain are using this selling as an opportunity to increase the gold content of their reserve positions.

In keeping with our view on forecasting the right direction, rather than timing or magnitude, we have avoided making an explicit forecast on the future price of gold. Our statistical studies going back to the nineteenth century lead us to conclude that the gold price should double to around $700 per ounce by the end of the decade. Our best guess is that a confluence of events, myths and perceptions will lead to the achievement of that price within the next three or four years.

Against this background, we make the case for gold as an asset to be used as part of an investment portfolio. In fact, its long-term performance (and short-term performance in many currencies) has earned it a place in the asset mix of every diversified portfolio.

Bullion is only one investment alternative. The investment and banking industries have developed hybrid securities and derivatives. Of course, gold mining companies come and go. In the preceding pages we have outlined the variety of ways that an investor can utilize any or all of these various instruments in order to achieve the proper use of gold as an asset class in a diversified investment portfolio.

We conclude that gold and its various investment products are complex and not well understood even within the professional investment community, let alone by lay investors. Thus, while we recommend the inclusion of gold in an individual's portfolio, we also recommend caution. Bullion will undoubtedly rise in price, and coins, wafers and bars are an alternative for the most conservative investors, or as part of a child's or grandchild's legacy. But bullion is only one alternative. As its price rises, options and futures will make fortunes for many people and paupers of others. While derivatives offer the highest potential returns, they also offer the highest risk of permanent capital loss. They are best left to sophisticated speculators who understand and who can afford the risk involved.

In the rising market that we foresee, shares will offer much better potential gains than bullion. But as we have pointed out, the analysis of gold mining stock involves much more than an examination of financial statements. Some companies will prove to be much better value than others, and at some specific times, bullion will prove to be better value than shares, as a group. The bullion and gold share markets are not fields for untrained beginners.

For the vast majority of investors, the best solution is a portfolio of bullion and gold shares as part of a larger portfolio encompassing other asset classes. Like the umbrella portfolio, the gold segment should be built, managed, and adjusted to reflect relative values and expected moves in the markets.

If you have the experience and skill to thoroughly analyze your alternatives and manage your portfolio on a continuous basis, by all means do so, because you have the attributes that will likely lead you to success. Otherwise choose one of the recognized gold investment professionals, either directly or through one or more of the open-end or closed-end gold funds offered in various U.S. and Canadian jurisdictions.

Glossary

Accumulation plans: Provided by fund dealers, brokers or fund managers, these plans allow investors to buy specific dollar amounts of a fund on a regular basis, i.e., monthly or quarterly. Also known as dollar-cost-averaging plans, automatic purchase plans, or preauthorized purchase plans.

Acquisition fees: Commissions charged for purchasing mutual fund units or shares.

Allocated account: An investment account that is separated from other investors' and the dealer's accounts; the opposite of an unallocated account.

Arbitrageurs: Professional traders whose earnings arise from spreads between different derivatives and investments.

Ask price: The price at which a seller is willing to part with an investment.

Assay: An analysis of the nature or purity of a metal, or its proportion in an ore body.

At-the-money: In options trading, a contract where the strike or exercise price is the same as the underlying investment's market price.

Automatic purchase plans: *See* Accumulation plans.

Bear market: The condition where a market is in a downward trend.

Bear spreading: In options trading, the practice of selling one option against another so as to benefit from price declines in the underlying investment.

Bid price: The price that a buyer is willing to pay for a particular investment.

Book value: The actual value of a company's assets as listed in its financial statements. Generally compared to share price to determine investment merit.

Bull market:

The condition where a market is in an upward trend.

Bullion:

A precious metal in its physical form, as opposed to a paper security or contract.

Call contract:

In options trading, a contract bestowing the right to purchase an investment such as stock or bullion at a certain price until a certain date.

Carat:

A measurement of the purity of gold; 24-carat gold is said to be 99.99 percent pure, whereas 18-carat gold is 75 percent pure. Minimum caratage varies by country, and ranges from 9 in Canada and England to 22 in some Mideast countries.

Central bank:

The financial institution that controls a country's fiscal policy by controlling its money supply.

Closed-end mutual funds:

Mutual funds that have a limit on the number of shares or units they can issue; once the limit is reached, the fund is closed to further investment, although the shares or units may still be traded through brokers.

Comex:	The New York Commodity Exchange.
Commodity markets:	Markets established for the trading of commodities such as silver and gold, as opposed to stocks or bonds.
Compound options:	The use of options on options to provide price protection; for example, a producing company might use a call on a put, paying a premium for the right to buy a put at a specific price.
Commissions:	Fees levied by a broker or fund manager for the purchase and/or sale of an investment.
Contango:	The difference between the spot price and futures price of a commodity. In the case of gold, this generally reflects carrying, storage, and insurance costs until the contract delivery month.
Convertibility:	The capability to be converted into another type of investment. For example, gold certificates may be convertible into gold bullion.
Coronas:	Austrian gold coins.

Covered writing: The practice of backing up a leveraged futures or options contract with an offsetting investment such as bullion or another contract.

Daily limit: In futures trading, the maximum price change permitted for a particular commodity or contract.

Debasing: The process of reducing the purity of a metal or currency.

Deflation: An economic scenario involving a general shrinking of prices for commodities and consumer goods; the opposite of inflation.

Delivery: As in "taking delivery" — in futures trading, the process of taking receipt of the underlying commodity rather than selling the contract prior to maturity.

Delta Hedge: A mechanism used by dealers to calculate appropriate gold trading levels to offset risk in hedging.

Derivatives: Products such as futures and options contracts that are derived from primary investments such as commodities or stocks.

Diversification:　　　　The practice of choosing diverse investments for a portfolio so as to reduce the effect of adverse price changes in any single investment area.

Dollar-cost-averaging plans:　　　　*See* Accumulation plans.

Eagles:　　　　American gold coins currently available in sizes of one ounce, half ounce, quarter ounce, and one-tenth ounce.

Exchanges:　　　　Clearing houses or markets for the trading of commodities, options, stocks, or other investments.

Exercise price:　　　　The price at which an options contract can be used or "exercised."

Expiry date:　　　　The date upon which an options contract ceases to have effect.

Fineness:　　　　A measurement of the purity of a precious metal. The highest fineness is .9999 (or 999.9) rather than 1.000, reflecting the fact that no metal can ever be absolutely pure.

Fix:　　　　The price at which gold's value is established in London at the "morning fix" and "afternoon fix."

Fixed-income assets: Interest-generating investments such as Canada Savings Bonds, Guaranteed Investment Certificates, term deposits, and treasury bills.

Flow-through limited partnerships: Special Canadian investment vehicles originally intended to promote investment in resource exploration through tax incentives. (Most of these tax incentives have now been eliminated.)

Forward selling: The practice by producers of selling their future production to secure operating capital and/or lock in prices.

Front-end load: With mutual funds, the same as an acquisition fee.

Futures contract: An obligation to buy or sell a certain amount of a particular commodity by a certain date.

Garimpeiros: Small independent Brazilian gold producers.

Gold bars: The standard unit of gold bullion, available in sizes of 1 kilogram, 100 ounces, or 400 ounces, or less.

Gold bug: Generally speaking, an individual who is bullish on gold.

Gold certificates: Paper securities issued by financial institutions as a convenient proxy for bullion, although they may not necessarily be backed by a corresponding amount of bullion in the institution's vault.

Gold loan: The practice of a financial institution lending gold rather than cash to a producer, then selling the gold on the producer's behalf to provide it with cash; the company subsequently repays the gold from future production.

Gold securities: Any of a number of paper investments directly or indirectly reflecting gold holdings, including certificates and stocks.

Gold stocks: Shares of gold-producing companies.

Gold wafers: Units of gold bullion, typically smaller than bars and ranging in size from 1 gram to 500 grams (or half an ounce to 10 ounces in Imperial measurements).

Good delivery: A standard by which deliveries of gold must be at least .995 pure to be acceptable on world markets.

Heap-leach technology:

A process that permits the economic extraction of gold from very low-grade ore deposits.

Hedging:

The practice of using derivatives to protect against adverse future price movements in an investment; can be likened to a form of investment insurance.

In-the-money:

In options trading, a contract that has intrinsic value is said to be in-the-money.

Inflation:

The economic phenomenon of generally increasing prices for commodities and consumer goods; economic theory cites monetary oversupply as the cause.

Intrinsic value:

In options trading, the amount by which the exercise or strike price differs from the market value of the underlying investment. With call options, intrinsic value is the amount by which the strike price exceeds market price; with put contracts, it is the amount by which the market value exceeds the exercise price.

Junior gold shares: The stock of small mining companies that may have just begun production; more speculative juniors may have no production as yet, just exploration rights on certain land areas, in which case they could be synonymous with penny mine stocks.

Krugerrands: South African gold coins.

Leverage: The ability to control a relatively large investment with a minimal amount of investment capital; typically, futures contracts provide leveraging of around 10 to 1, meaning you can control $10 worth of assets with only a dollar of your own money.

Liquidity: A measure of the freedom with which an investment can be liquidated, or turned into cash.

Loco London: An expression used to denote the price of gold as delivered to London.

Long: In futures or options trading, a position where an investor has an obligation or right to buy as opposed to sell an underlying investment; the opposite of a short position.

Management fees: Ongoing fees charged by mutual funds for managing their investments. Generally expressed as an annual percentage of assets.

Maple Leafs: Canadian gold coins. Currently available in $50, $20, $10, and $5 denominations containing one ounce, half ounce, quarter ounce, and one-tenth ounce of .9999 (999.9) fineness gold respectively.

Margin: In futures trading, the amount of money required to cover a contract.

Naked contract: In options or futures trading, a contract that is not offset by the ownership of non-leveraged assets. The opposite of a covered contract.

Napoleons: French gold coins.

**Net asset value per
share:**   The total value of assets in a mutual fund, net of any liabilities, divided by the number of shares outstanding.

Net present value: In the case of a gold producing company, the sum of its gold and other assets, less corporate debt.

Nugget: Australian gold coin.

Numismatic value: The scarcity value of a coin, as opposed to the value of the bullion it contains.

Open contract: A contract that is still outstanding. For example, a put option would be an open contract until it has expired or been exercised. A futures "buy" contract would be open until an offsetting "sell" contract is purchased, or delivery is taken.

Open-end mutual funds: Mutual funds with no restriction on the amount of shares that they may issue.

Opening price: The price fixed by an exchange at the opening of trading.

Option contracts: Contracts bestowing the right to buy or sell an investment at a certain price until a certain date.

Option premium: The price paid for an option. It reflects the intrinsic value of the option, as well as its time or speculative value.

Option writer: A party who undertakes an obligation to fulfill an options contract if it is exercised.

Out-of-the-money: An options contract that has no intrinsic value. Opposite of in-the-money.

Penny mine stocks: Highly speculative shares of small exploration companies with no actual production.

Position: Investment stance; for example, someone who owns bullion or rights or obligations to buy bullion is said to be in a long position; someone who has an obligation or right to sell bullion without actually owning any bullion is said to be in a short position.

Preauthorized purchase plans: *See* Accumulation plans.

Premium: In options trading, the cost of a contract. In bullion trading, the extra cost placed on a wafer or bar to cover handling, shipping, etc.

Price to earnings ratio: A measurement of a stock's value based on its relationship to annual earnings. The price to cash flow ratio is a variation also used to measure stock value.

Prospectus: Explanatory documentation that mutual funds are legally required to provide to prospective investors. The nature and content of this documentation can vary somewhat, depending on the jurisdiction in which the investment is sold.

Put contracts: In options trading, the right to sell a certain amount of a particular investment at a certain price until the expiry date.

Real value: The long-term historical value of gold, after inflation is taken into account.

Rear-end load: The same as the redemption fee.

Redemption fees: Charges levied by mutual fund managers for selling fund units. Funds charging these fees generally do not charge acquisition fees.

Segregated account: Same as allocated account.

Short selling: The process of acquiring rights or obligations to sell a particular investment without owning the investment itself. The opposite of going long.

Sovereigns: British gold coins.

Speculative value: In options trading, the premium placed on an investment's current value, based on market sentiment as to its future value.

Spot price: The current price for a commodity, as established by a particular exchange or by the spot market.

Spread: Generally speaking, the difference between any two prices; for example, the spread between spot prices and future prices, or the spread between a call option strike price and the market price.

Spreading: The practice of selling one option against another.

Stop-loss orders: Instructions to brokers to liquidate a position if adverse price moves exceed a specified limit.

Straddle: The purchase of call and put contracts simultaneously to guard against large price swings in either direction. In some cases, speculators may enter into straddles to benefit from the changing spread between call and put prices.

Strike price: Same as the exercise price in options trading.

Swaption: The practice of issuing the rights to sell fixed amounts of gold at a predetermined price over a series of future dates.

Time value: In options trading, the same as speculative value.

Unallocated account: An account in which one's assets are pooled with those of other investors and possibly the dealer.

Up-and-out option: A put option that automatically expires if the price of the under-lying investment moves upward beyond a certain level.

Variability: The tendency and extent to which an investment fluctuates in price.

Volatility: Same as variability.

Index

accumulation plans, 179-81
acquisition fees, 175-76
Age of Diminished Expectations, 42
Alberta: buying coins, 129
American Barrick, 68, 156
Australia: gold loans, 82; hedging, 84; mine production, 62, 72

Bank of Canada, 36
Bank of England, 21, 22, 78
Bank of Nova Scotia, 131, 134, 138
Black-Scholes model, 193
Brazil: gold hoarding, 5; mine production, 62, 73
Bretton Woods Conference, 23
Britain: gold exchange standard, 19, 20; introduction of gold standard, 12, 16; jewelry, 91; value of pound in 1920s, 21
bullion: as an investment, 4-5, 116, 128-30, 209; bars and wafers, 130-33; certificates, 133-35; coins, 78, 95-96, 129, 135-38; in London market, 55-57

call options, 122, 191, 197-99
Canada: exploration, 71-72; fees charged by fund companies, 176-78; gold holdings, 80; gold mutual funds, 162, 163, 168, 171; gold sales by central bank, 208; government spending policies, 24; jewelry, 91; Maple Leaf coins, 95, 135-36; mine production, 62; purchases of gold bullion and gold coins, 129-30; reduced inflation rates, 29, 31
Canadian Imperial Bank of Commerce, 138
capital gain tax, 129

Capitalism: The Unknown Ideal, 39
caratage, 91-92
cash flow, 144, 152-54
central banks. *See* banking system
certificates, 133-35, 138
Chicago Board of Trade, 187
Chicago Mercantile Exchange, 187
China: mine production, 75
closed-end funds, 121
coins: bullion, 78, 95-96, 129, 135-38; certificates, 138; numismatic, 125-26
commission charges, 132, 134, 137-38
commodity: gold as a, 58-59
commodity exchanges: gold futures contracts, 187
Commonwealth of Independent States: demand for jewelry, 91; depleted gold reserves, 109, 208; inflation, 205; mine production, 62, 73-76; need to attract investment; 97-98; political unrest, 50
contango, 82, 85, 147, 186
Credit Anstalt, 22
credit deflation, 44-45

dealer: choosing, to buy and sell gold, 138-39
debt monetization, 204-5
delta hedge, 87-88
demographic patterns, 31-32, 43
derivatives, 2-3, 61, 99, 121-24, 184-202, 209
diversification: gold mutual fund, 164
due diligence examination, 149-51

Eastern bloc countries: inflation,

205; sales and production, 73-
76, 80
economic history, 2, 9-12;
introduction of gold standard,
16-18; 1920s and 1930s, 18-23;
postwar years, 23-25
environmental concerns, 69-70
European Economic Community,
50
European economy: 1880s to
1914, 17-18; 1920s, 20-21;
1930s, 22
European Options Exchange, 191
exploration: decisions, 64-76;
junior exploration companies,
141-42; North America, 70-72;
penny mines, 124-25

Federal Reserve Bank, 30, 36, 78
financial analysis of mining
company, 151-54
financial asset: gold as a, 58
First World War, 12, 17
flow-through limited partnership,
71-72
foreign-exchange reserves, 18, 21,
78
forward sales, 49, 81-82, 84-89
France: caratage for jewelry, 91-
92; inflation in 1920s, 21
free-market economy, 14
fund management companies:
accumulation plans, 179-81;
fees, 175-78; withdrawal plan,
181
funds: advantage for investor,
156; closed-end funds, 121, 162,
166-68; manager, 172-74;
mutual gold funds, 121, 162-66;
portfolio, 170-78; protection for,
169; selecting a gold fund, 169-
70
future contracts, 2, 121-24, 145-
46, 185-90

Germany: costs of unification, 33,
205; economy in 1920s and
1930s, 18, 21, 22

gold exchange standard, 18-23
Gold Fields Mineral Services, 74,
75, 79, 84
gold standard, 12, 16-18, 62-63
government: spending policies,
24; use of gold as investment,
108-09
Great Depression, 22-23
Greenspan, Alan, 38-39

hard currency countries, 20
heap-leach technologies, 69, 72
hedging, 81, 107-08, 145
holdings: world gold, 78, 80

in-the-money option, 191-92
India: jewelry, 92
inflation: cost of, 27-31; economic
history, 9, 10, 12-16, 20-21; gold
exchange standard, 20; in 1970s
and 1980s, 25-26, 30; in 1990s,
31-33, 43, 45-46, 203-06; price
of gold, 107-08, 112; real value
of gold, 34-41; South Africa, 66-
67; value of gold in times of, 27-
28, 206
interest rates, 25, 30, 32, 96, 108
International Monetary Fund, 23,
79
International Operations Clearing
Corporation, 191
international trade, 17-18
intrinsic value, 191-92
Iran: gold sales, 80
Iraq: gold sales, 80
Italy: caratage for jewelry, 91-92

Japan: economy in 1990s, 33, 50,
205; gold reserves, 79, 109-10;
jewelry, 92-93
jewelry: demand for gold, 48, 76,
90-94, 99, 109
junior exploration companies,
141-42

Lac Minerals, 185
Latin America: mine production,
73

liquidity, 21-22, 156, 165-66
loans: gold, 81-82, 146-48
London gold market, 55-57

MacArthur-Forrest process, 63
management fee, 162, 174, 177
Maple Leaf coins, 126, 135-36
Mexico: gold coins, 95
Mid-America Exchange, 187, 191
mine production: Australia, 72;
   China, 75; decisions, 64-76;
   former Soviet Union and Eastern
   bloc countries, 73-75; hedging,
   83-84; history of, 62-64; in
   1990s, 206-07; Latin America,
   73; North America, 64-66, 68-
   72, 118-19; Papua New Guinea,
   72-73; South Africa, 66-68
money: concept of sound money,
   14-15; effect of inflation, 13-16;
   paper, 12, 16, 21, 27-28, 108-
   09; supply, 13-19, 24, 204
Montreal Exchange, 191
mutual funds. See funds

Nevada: buying coins, 129; heap-
   leach technologies, 69; net
   profits tax, 72
New Deal, 35
New Guinea Mining, 73
New York Commodity Exchange
   (Comex), 57, 84, 122, 187, 190-
   91
no-load funds, 175
North America: bullion coins,
   129, 135; gold loans, 82; gold
   shares, 118-19, 141, 155;
   hedging, 84; inflation, 203-05;
   jewelry, 93; mine production,
   62-64, 68-72, 118-19; money
   supply, 13-15; trading gold
   futures, 187; valuation of gold
   equities, 143
Northwest Gold, 68
numismatic coins, 125-26

open-end shares, 163
option contracts: 2, 87-88, 121-

23, 184, 190-202; average price
   options, 88; call options, 122,
   191, 197-99; out-of-the money
   put options, 87, 191-92; over-
   the-counter options, 88; put
   options, 122, 191, 199-200;
   straddle strategy, 201-02

panic buying, 49, 50
paper money, 12, 16, 21, 27-28,
   108-09
Papua New Guinea, 72-73
penny mines, 124-25
Persian Gulf War, 3-5, 84, 107-08
Philadelphia Exchange, 185
Placer Dome, 68, 185
placer mines, 75
portfolio: inclusion of gold in,
   155-66, 170-78, 209-10
premium, 122, 191-92
professional investment
   management, 161-66
property visit, 149-51
put options, 122, 191, 199-200

recession, 15, 25, 32-33, 93
recycling: old gold scrap, 76, 78
redemption fees, 175-78
Republic National Bank of New
   York, 136
reserve currencies, 18-20, 23, 79,
   109-10
reserves: foreign exchange, 18,
   21, 78; gold, 3, 16-18, 74, 208;
   of mining company, 149-50
return: from bullion and mining
   shares, 116-17; rate of, 110-11
risk: gold as an investment, 110,
   111, 113; gold futures contracts,
   190; options, 193-94

sales: forward selling, 49, 81-82,
   84-89; from central banks, 78-
   80, 98-99; from former Soviet
   Union and Eastern bloc
   countries, 73-75, 98; spot
   deferred sales, 81-82, 85-86; tax
   on coins, 129, 135

Saudi Arabia; jewelry, 92
scrap: old gold, 76, 78, 99
shares: advantage of a portfolio,
   155-60; analyzing gold, 149-54;
   investing in gold, 116-21, 140-
   43, 209; price to earnings and
   price to cash flow multiples,
   144-48
sound money, 14-15
South Africa: arrangements with
   Rothschild's, 55; gold coins, 95,
   136-37; gold share market, 118,
   141, 155; hedging, 82, 85; mine
   production, 62-64, 66-68;
   political turmoil, 50, 207
South African Reserve Bank, 85
Southeast Asia: jewelry, 92
Soviet Union. See Commonwealth
   of Independent States
Spain: gold reserves, 208
Spanish conquest of the
   Americas, 11-12
speculators, 2, 60, 71, 117, 122-
   23, 142, 188-89, 194
spot deferred sales, 81-82, 85-86
spot price, 82, 86-88, 186
stock exchange: trading options,
   185, 190-91
storage accounts, 133
storage and administration
   charges, 134, 138
strike price, 191
Switzerland: gold reserves, 79
Sydney Stock Exchange, 191

Taiwan: gold reserves, 80, 208;
   jewelry, 92
Thailand: jewelry, 92
time value of option, 192
Tokyo Commodity Exchange, 187

Toronto Dominion Bank, 138
Trans Canada Options Inc., 185
Turkey: jewelry, 92

unemployment, 30, 31, 42, 43
United States: actions to end
   recession, 32-33; economy
   1920s to 1960s, 21-23;
   economic forecast for 1990s, 42-
   46; fees charged by fund
   companies, 175-77; gold as an
   investment, 96-97; gold coins,
   95, 136; gold exchange
   standard, 19; gold mutual funds,
   168; gold reserves, 79;
   government spending policies,
   24; inflation in 1970s and
   1980s, 25-26, 30; inflation in
   1990s, 43, 205; jewelry, 91, 92;
   mine production, 62;
   nationalized gold, 22; Persian
   Gulf War, 84, 107-08; price of
   gold, 35-36; reliance on free
   markets, 28-29
U.S. Consumer Price Index, 34
U.S. Wholesale Price Index, 34

valuation of gold equities, 143-48;
   of mining company, 151-54
value investing, 119
Vancouver Stock Exchange, 71,
   125, 191
variability, 112-13

weight: bullion bars and wafers,
   130-32
Winnipeg Exchange, 184
World Gold Council, 48, 72, 73,
   75-76, 93-94

Zurich gold market, 57